Study Guide

Marketing

Second Edition

Study Guide
Charles W. Beem
Bucks County Community College

Marketing
Real People
Real Choices

Michael R. Solomon
Elnora W. Stuart

Prentice Hall
Upper Saddle River, NJ 07458

Acquisitions editor: *Leah Johnson*
Associate editor: *John Larkin*
Project editor: *Theresa Festa*
Manufacturer: *Quebecor Printing Group*

Printed in the United States of America

10   9   8   7   6   5   4   3   2   1

ISBN 0-13-013627-1

Prentice-Hall International (UK) Limited, *London*
Prentice-Hall of Australia Pty. Limited, *Sydney*
Prentice-Hall Canada Inc., *Toronto*
Prentice-Hall Hispanoamericana, S.A., *Mexico*
Prentice-Hall of India Private Limited, *New Delhi*
Prentice-Hall of Japan, Inc., *Tokyo*
Prentice-Hall (Singapore) Pte Ltd
Editora Prentice-Hall do Brasil, Ltda., *Rio de Janeiro*

TABLE OF CONTENTS

CHAPTER 1:   Welcome To The World of Marketing 1
CHAPTER 2:   Strategic Planning: Making Choices in a Dynamic
              Environment 15
CHAPTER 3:   Decision Making In The New Era of Marketing:
              Enriching the Marketing Environment 29
CHAPTER 4:   Think Globally and Act Locally: Marketing In a
              Multinational Environment 44
CHAPTER 5:   Marketing Information and Research: Analyzing the
              Business Environment 59
CHAPTER 6:   Why People Buy: Consumer Behavior 72
CHAPTER 7:   Why Organizations Buy: Business-To-Business
              Markets 85
CHAPTER 8:   Sharpening the Focus:
              Target Marketing Strategies 98
CHAPTER 9:   The Product 111
CHAPTER 10:   Product Management 124
CHAPTER 11:   Broadening the Product Focus:
              Marketing Intangibles and Services 137
CHAPTER 12:   Pricing the Product 149
CHAPTER 13:   Pricing Methods 161
CHAPTER 14:   Channel Management, Wholesaling, and Physical
              Distribution: Delivering the Product 173
CHAPTER 15:   Retailing and Direct Marketing: Buying
              the Product 187
CHAPTER 16:   The Promotion Superhighway 200
CHAPTER 17:   Advertising 214
CHAPTER 18:   Sales Promotion, Public Relations,
              and Personal Selling 227

TO THE STUDENT

The purpose of this study guide is to aid you in more effectively learning the material in Marketing by Solomon and Stuart.

This study guide is designed and written to reinforce your learning from the textbook, class, lectures, and class discussions. The objectives of this study guide are:

1.   to provide you with the materials that will be useful in learning the business vocabulary and business concepts presented in your text.

2.   to provide you with an opportunity to test your understanding of what you have read, studies, and learned.

3.   to help you prepare for quizzes and examinations by testing yourself with sample exam-type questions.

4.   to encourage you to apply your understanding of the business concepts presented in the text to interesting, real-world business problems and opportunities.

THE ORGANIZATION OF THE STUDY GUIDE

Each chapter in this Study Guide is arranged in the following order:

1. **Chapter Overview:** The short chapter summary will help you to review the basic important elements of each chapter.

2. **Learning Objectives:** The learning objectives are listed (as they appear in the beginning of each text chapter) to provide an organized structural framework of the chapter.

3. **Chapter Outline:** The chapter outline requires you to define, list or describe the business concepts as related to the fulfillment of each of the chapters' learning objectives. The textbook page numbers are provided in order to help guide you through this learning exercise.

4. **Key Terms:** This practice exercise will allow you to test your knowledge of some of the important terms provided in your textbook.

5. **Multiple Choice:** The Multiple Choice questions were written and designed to measure your understanding of the chapter and to prepare you for course examinations.

6. **Chapter In Review—Writing To Learn:** This exercise provides an excellent opportunity for you to practice and develop your writing skills, while reviewing what you have learned. Enjoy the challenge as you build your confidence.

7. **A Case Analysis Exercise:** Reread the Opening Vignette as presented at the beginning of each chapter of your textbook. Apply what you have learned in reading and studying the chapter to answer the questions provided.

8. **Answers:** Answers are provided for each learning exercise, including an outline for each chapter.

SPECIAL ACKNOWLEDGEMENTS

I would like to begin by thanking Don Hull, Senior Editor at Prentice Hall for allowing me the privilege to contribute my work in preparing this Study Guide to accompany the very excellent textbook, Marketing, by Solomon and Stuart. I am also grateful to John Larkin, Assistant Editor, Business, of Prentice Hall for the many useful suggestions provided to me while working on this Study Guide. Others I wish to thank include my wonderful wife, Karen, and my father, John R. Beem, M.D., who has guided and inspired me to pursue my career in teaching.

This Study Guide is dedicated to my loving wife, Karen, for her support and understanding.

Good Luck!

Charles W. Beem
Bucks County Community College
Newtown, Pennsylvania
(215) 968-8237

CHAPTER 1

WELCOME TO THE WORLD OF MARKETING

CHAPTER OVERVIEW

Marketing is the process of planning and executing the conception, pricing, promotion, and distribution of ideas, goods, and services to create exchanges that satisfy individual and organizational objectives.

The marketing mix includes four tools used to create the desired response from consumer and business markets. These four tools include product, price, place, and promotion. Marketers design the marketing mix so that consumers and business consumers will seek to exchange or trade money or something else of value for the product.

The strategic process of marketing planning begins with an assessment of factors within the organization and in the external environment that will help or hinder the development and marketing of products. Based on this analysis, marketing objectives are set and strategies are developed.

Next, we explored the evolution of the marketing concept. Early in this century, companies followed a production orientation, followed by a sales orientation, then a consumer orientation, (which led to the widespread adoption of the marketing concept), and finally today, where many firms are moving toward a New Era orientation that includes not only a commitment to quality but also concern for both economic and social profit.

We also discovered how the marketing system is important to individual and business customers in the marketplace, in our daily lives, and in society. Specifically we considered the concept of utility -- that is, the usefulness or benefit provided by a product. Four kinds of utility in marketing include form utility, place utility, time utility, and possession utility.

Finally we explained marketing's role within an organization. Please remember that marketing decisions cannot be made in isolation from an organization's other operations, so that marketing, finance, manufacturing, research and development, and other functional areas must work together to achieve the organization's goals.

CHAPTER OBJECTIVES

1. Define the marketing concept.

2. Describe the marketing mix.

3. Understand the basics of marketing planning.

4. Describe the evolution of the marketing concept.

5. Explain how marketing is important to both individual and business customers in the marketplace, in our daily lives, and in society.

6. Explain marketing's role within an organization.

CHAPTER OUTLINE

Please refer to your textbook in order to define, list, and/or describe the missing parts of the chapter outline. The page numbers given will help guide you through this learning process.

I. WHAT IS MARKETING?
    Marketing _____ *(p.3)*
    A. Marketing Satisfies Needs _____ *(p.3)*
        Consumer _____ *(p.3)*
        1. The Marketing Concept _____
            _____ *(p.3)*
            Need _____ *(p.4)*
            Want _____ *(p.4)*
            Benefit _____ *(p.4)*
            Demand _____ *(p.4)*
            Market _____ *(p.4)*
            Marketplace _____ *(p.4)*
        2. Satisfying Society's Needs, Too
            Social Marketing Concept _____
            _____ *(p.5)*

    B. Marketing Is an Exchange of Value _____
        _____ *(p.5)*
        Exchange _____ *(p.5)*

    C. (Almost) Anything Can Be Marketed
        Product _____ *(p.6)*
        1. Consumer Goods and Services
            Consumer Goods _____ *(p.6)*
            Services _____ *(p.6)*
        2. Business-to-Business Marketing
            Industrial Goods _____ *(p.6)*
        3. Not-for-Profit Marketing _____
            _____ *(p.6)*

     4.   Idea, Place and People Marketing _____ *(p.7)*

     5.   Marketing Sports, Entertainment, and Places ___ *(p.8)*

  D.   Marketing's Tools: The Marketing Mix _____ *(p.9)*

     1.   Product _____ *(p.9)*
     2.   Price _____ *(p.10)*
     3.   Place _____ *(p.10)*
     4.   Promotion _____ *(p.10)*

  E.   Marketing is a Process _____ *(p.10)*

    Relationship Marketing _____ *(p.10)*

II. HOW IS MARKETING DONE? _____ *(P.10)*

  A.   Marketing Planning _____ *(p.12)*

    Mass Market _____ *(p.12)*

  B.   Finding and Reaching a Target Market
    Market Segment _____ *(p.12)*
    Target Market _____ *(p.12)*
     1.   Segmenting the Market _____ *(p.13)*

     2.   Selecting a Target Market _____ *(p.13)*

     3.   Positioning the Product _____ *(p.13)*

III. WHEN DID MARKETING BEGIN: THE EVOLUTION OF A CONCEPT
  A.   The Production Orientation _____ *(p.14)*

  B.   The Selling Orientation _____ *(p.15)*

  C.   The Consumer Orientation _____ *(p.16)*

  D.   The New Era Orientation _____ *(p.17)*

IV. WHY IS MARKETING IMPORTANT? _____ *(p.17)*

  A.   Marketing Creates Utility
    Utility _____ *(p.17)*
    Form Utility _____ *(p.17)*
    Place Utility _____ *(p.17)*
    Time Utility _____ *(p.17)*

Possession Utility _____ *(p.17)*

B.   Marketing's Role in the Firm _____
     _____ *(p.18)*

C.   Marketing's Role in Our Daily Lives: Opera to Oprah
     1.   Popular Culture _____
          _____ *(p.18)*
     2.   Marketing and Myths _____
          _____ *(p.18)*

D.   Marketing's Role in Society _____
     _____ *(p.19)*
     1.   Ethical Behavior in Good Business _____
          _____ *(p.19)*
     2.   Social and Ethical Criticisms of Marketing _____
          _____ *(p.20)*

CHAPTER 1

KEY TERMS
Select the correct term for each definition and write it in the space provided.

Benefit   Demand
Consumer orientation   Marketing
Want   Popular Culture
Market   Target Market
Consumer   Need
Relationship marketing   Product
Marketing concept   Mass market
Utility

1.   _Marketing_   The process of planning and executing the
                              conception, pricing, promotion, and
                              distribution of ideas, goods, and
                              services to create exchanges that satisfy
                              individual organizational objectives.
                              (p.3)

2.   _Consumer_   The ultimate user of a purchased good or
                              service. *(p.3)*

X 3.   _Consumer Orientation_   A management orientation that focuses on
                              identifying and satisfying consumer needs
                              in order to assure the organization's
                              long-term profitability objectives. *(p.3)*

4

4. _Need_ — Recognition of any difference between a consumer's actual state and some ideal or desired state. *(p.4)*

5. _Want_ — The desire to satisfy needs in specific ways that are culturally and socially influenced. *(p.4)*

6. _Demand_ — Customers' desire for products coupled with the resources to obtain them. *(p.4)*

7. _Benefit_ — The outcome sought by a customer that motivates buying behavior. *(p.4)*

8. _Market_ — All of the customers and potential customers who share a common need that can be satisfied by a specific product, who have the resources to exchange for it, who are willing to make the exchange, and who have the authority to make the exchange. *(p.4)*

9. _Product_ — A good, service, idea, place or person offered in the exchange process to satisfy consumer or business customer needs and wants. *(p.9)*

10. _Relationship Marketing_ — A marketing philosophy that focuses on building long-term relationships with customers to satisfy mutual needs. *(p.10)*

11. _Mass Market_ — All possible customers in a market, regardless of the differences in their specific needs and wants. *(p.12)*

12. _Target market_ — The market segment(s) on which an organization focuses its marketing plan and toward which it directs its marketing efforts. *(p.12)*

X 13. _Marketing Concept_ — A management philosophy that focuses on ways to satisfy customers' needs and wants. *(p.16)*

14. _Utility_ — The usefulness or benefit received by consumers from a product. *(p.17)*

15. _Pop Culture_ — The music, movies, sports, books, celebrities, and other forms of entertainment consumed by the mass market. *(p.18)*

MULTIPLE CHOICE
Identify the most correct answer.

1. The outcome that occurs when a product satisfies a need is known as a: *(p.4)*
    a. want.
    b. demand.
    c. benefit.
    d. utility.

2. An orientation that focuses on satisfying consumer needs while also addressing the needs of the larger society is the: *(p.5)*
    a. community marketing concept.
    b. social marketing concept.
    c. environmental marketing concept.
    d. consumer marketing concept.

3. In order for an exchange to occur,: *(p.5)*
    a. at least two people or organizations must be willing to make a trade.
    b. both parties must agree on the value of the exchange and how it will be carried out.
    c. each party must be free to accept or reject the other's offer.
    d. all of the above.

4. Goods bought by individuals or organizations for further processing or for use in doing business are: *(p.6)*
    a. consumer goods.
    b. industrial goods.
    c. the marketing mix.
    d. processed goods.

5. The elements in the marketing mix are: *(p.9)*
    a. product, price, promotion, and place.
    b. need, product, satisfaction, and supply.
    c. goods, service, product, and place.
    d. planning, pricing, promotion, and distribution.

6. The amount the consumer must exchange in order to receive the offering is the: *(p.10)*
    a. demand.
    b. profit.
    c. price.
    d. resource.

7. The series of firms that work together to get a product from a producer to a consumer are known as: *(p.10)*
    a. channels of distribution.
    b. intermediary firms.
    c. mass production.
    d. relationship marketing.

8. Promotion includes all of the marketing activities that are designed to encourage potential customers to buy the product and can take many forms, including: *(p.10)*
   a. personal selling.
   b. television advertising.
   c. store coupons.
   d. all of the above.

9. The first phase of the marketing planning processes involves: *(p.12)*
   a. reaching a target market.
   b. analyzing the organization's current strengths and weaknesses.
   c. positioning the product.
   d. segmenting the market.

10. The aim of a positioning strategy is to: *(p.13)*
   a. evaluate the segments identified in the segmentation process.
   b. focus on reaching as many customers as possible.
   c. obtain a competitive advantage over competing products in the minds of consumers.
   d. none of the above.

11. Management philosophy that emphasizes the most efficient ways to produce and distribute products is known as: *(p.14)*
   a. product orientation.
   b. marketing concept.
   c. product strategy
   d. production management.

12. Federal Express began overnight delivery services in: *(p.15)*
   a. 1962.
   b. 1971.
   c. 1973.
   d. 1979.

13. New Era orientation is: *(p.17)*
   a. a management philosophy in future marketing.
   b. a management philosophy in which marketing decision making means a devotion to excellence in designing and producing products and creating products that benefit the customer plus the firm's employees, shareholders, and fellow citizens.
   c. a management philosophy that emphasizes aggressive sales practices and marketing is seen strictly as a sales function.
   d. a management philosophy that focuses on new wave thinking.

14. The consumer benefit provided when organizations make products available where customers want them is: *(p.17)*
    a. form utility.
    b. time utility.
    c. possession utility.
    d. place utility.

15. Marketing messages often communicate stories containing symbolic elements that express the shared emotions and ideals of a culture known as: *(p.18)*
    a. myths.
    b. product essays.
    c. Morse code.
    d. artificial legends.

CHAPTER IN REVIEW - WRITING TO LEARN

1. Describe how marketers plan and develop strategies for finding and reaching a market.

   _____

   _____

   _____

2. Explain the evolution of the marketing concept.

   _____

   _____

   _____

3. Explain marketing's role in the firm.

   _____

   _____

   _____

A Case Analysis Exercise

Real People, Real Choices: Meet Steve Goldstein, Levi Strauss

Reread the Opening Vignette on page 2 of your text and answer the following questions.

1. Who is Steve Goldstein?

2. Who does the advertising for Levi Strauss & Co.?

3. Discuss what it is that makes each of the Levi brands unique.

4. Discuss Steve Goldstein's marketing tasks.

5. Identify the Levi's brand product lines.

ANSWERS
CHAPTER OUTLINE

I. WHAT IS MARKETING?
Marketing--The process of planning and executing the conception, pricing, promotion, and distribution of ideas, goods, and services to create exchanges that satisfy individual and organizational objectives.
   A. Marketing Satisfies Needs--Marketing involves at least two parties--a seller and a buyer--each of whom have needs. Products are bought to satisfy consumer's needs.
   Consumer--The ultimate user of a purchased good or service.
      1. The Marketing Concept--A management orientation that focuses on identifying and satisfying consumer needs in order to assure the organization's long-term profitability objectives.
      Need--Recognition of any difference between a consumer's actual state and some ideal or desired state.
      Want--The desire to satisfy needs in specific ways that are culturally and socially influenced.
      Benefit--The outcome that occurs when a product satisfies a need.
      Demand--Customers' desire for products coupled with the resources to obtain them.
      Market--All of the customers and potential customers who share a common need that can be satisfied by a specific product, who have the resources to exchange for it, who are willing to make the exchange, and who have the authority to make the exchange.
      Marketplace--Any location or medium used to conduct an exchange.
      2. Satisfying Society's Needs, Too
      Social Marketing Concept--An orientation that focuses on satisfying consumer needs while also addressing the needs of a larger society.

   B. Marketing is an Exchange of Value--The buyer receives an object, service, or idea that satisfies a need, for which the seller receives something he or she feels is of equivalent value.
   Exchange--The process by which some transfer of value occurs between a buyer and a seller.

C. (Almost) Anything Can Be Marketed.
    Product--A good, service, idea, place, or person offered
    in the exchange process to satisfy consumer or business
    customer needs and wants.
    1. Consumer Goods and Services
        Consumer Goods--The goods purchased by individual
        consumers for personal or family use.
        Services--Intangible products that are exchanged
        directly from the producer to the customer.
    2. Business-to-Business Marketing
        Industrial Goods--Goods bought by individuals or
        organizations for further use in doing business.
    3. Not-for-Profit Marketing-- Museums, churches,
        charities, and hospitals are now practicing the
        marketing concept.
    4. Idea, Place, and People Marketing--Many of the
        famous people that you pay to see in concerts,
        stadiums, movies, etc. have been successfully
        marketed.
    5. Marketing Sports, Entertainment, and Places--Sports
        and entertainment activities do not just happen;
        they must be carefully planned. Places can also be
        marketed.

D. Marketing's Tools: The Marketing Mix--Consisting of the
    factors that can be manipulated and used together to
    create a desired response in the marketplace.
    1. Product--A good, service, idea, place, person--
        whatever is being offered for sale in the marketing
        exchange process.
    2. Price--The assignment of value, or the amount the
        consumer must exchange in order to receive the
        offering.
    3. Place--The availability of the product to the
        consumer at the time and location where it is
        desired, (channels of distribution).
    4. Promotion--The efforts by a marketer to inform or
        persuade consumers or organizations about goods,
        services, or ideas.

E. Marketing is a Process--It involves a series of steps
    that entail both careful thought (planning) and action
    (executing).
    Relationship Marketing--A marketing philosophy that
    focuses on building long-term relationships with
    customers to satisfy mutual needs.

II. HOW IS MARKETING DONE?--Marketing is a strategic decision
    process, in which marketing managers determine what marketing
    strategies will be used to help the organization meet its long
    term objectives.

A. Marketing Planning--Involves analyzing the organization's current situation. Specifically this takes into account the threats and opportunities in the marketplace, actions of competitors, cultural and technological changes, the economy, etc.
Mass Market--All possible customers in a market, regardless of the differences in their specific needs and wants.

B. Finding and Reaching a Target Market
Market Segment--A distinct group of customers within a larger market who are similar to one another in some way and whose needs differ from other customers in the larger market.
Target Market--The market segment(s) on which an organization focuses its marketing plan and toward which it directs its marketing efforts.
1. Segmenting the Market--The process of dividing the overall market into segments, where the consumers in each segment have one or more important characteristics in common, setting them apart from others.
2. Selecting a Target Market--The process of evaluating the segments in terms of relative attractiveness and profitability potential against the organization's resources and ability to satisfy the needs of the segments.
3. Positioning the Product--The aim of a positioning strategy is to obtain a competitive advantage over competing products in the minds of consumers.

III. WHEN DID MARKETING BEGIN: THE EVOLUTION OF A CONCEPT
A. The Production Orientation--A management philosophy that emphasizes the most efficient ways to produce and distribute products.

B. The Selling Orientation--A management philosophy that emphasizes aggressive sales practices and marketing is seen strictly as a sales function.

C. The Consumer Orientation--A management philosophy that focuses on ways to satisfy customers' needs and wants.

D. The New Era Orientation--A management philosophy in which marketing decision making means a devotion to excellence in designing and producing products and creating products that benefit the customer plus the firm's employees, shareholders, and fellow citizens.

IV. WHY IS MARKETING IMPORTANT?--Marketing principles are important to small business people, major corporations, homemakers, etc.

A. Marketing Creates Utility
    Utility--The usefulness or benefit received by consumers from a product.
    Form Utility--The consumer benefit provided by organizations when they change raw materials into finished products desired by consumers.
    Place Utility--The consumer benefit provided when organizations make products available where and when customers want them.
    Time Utility--The consumer benefit provided by storing products until they are needed by buyers.
    Possession Utility--The consumer benefits provided by an organization when they allow the consumer to own, use, and/or enjoy the product.

B. Marketing's Role in the Firm--Marketing managers must work with financial and accounting officers, and people involved in manufacturing.

C. Marketing's Role in Our Daily Lives: Opera to Oprah
    1. Popular Culture--The music, movies, sports, books, celebrities, and other forms of entertainment consumed by the mass market.
    2. Marketing and Myths--Marketing messages often communicate myths, stories containing symbolic elements that express the shared emotions and ideals of a culture.

D. Marketing's Role in Society--We rely on marketers to sell us products that are safe and perform as promised, to tell us the truth about what they are selling, and to price and distribute these products fairly.
    1. Ethical Behavior is Good Business--Companies usually find that stressing ethics and social responsibility is also good business, at least in the long run.
    2. Social and Ethical Criticisms of Marketing--Whether intentionally or not, some marketers do violate their bond of trust with consumers.

CHAPTER 1
ANSWERS

KEY TERMS	MULTIPLE CHOICE

KEY TERMS

1. Marketing
2. Consumer
3. Marketing concept
4. Need
5. Want
6. Demand
7. Benefit
8. Market
9. Product
10. Relationship marketing
11. Mass market
12. Target market
13. Consumer orientation
14. Utility
15. Popular culture

MULTIPLE CHOICE

1. c
2. b
3. d
4. b
5. a
6. c
7. a
8. d
9. b
10. c
11. a
12. c
13. b
14. d
15. a

CHAPTER IN REVIEW - WRITING TO LEARN

1. The strategic process of marketing planning begins with an assessment of factors within the organization and in the external environment that will help or hinder the development and marketing of products. Based on this analysis, marketing objectives are set and strategies are developed. Many firms use a target marketing strategy in which the overall market is divided into segments and the most attractive is targeted. Then the marketing mix is strategically designed to gain a competitive position in the target market.

2. Early in this century, companies followed a production orientation in which they focused on the most efficient ways to produce and distribute products. Beginning in the 1930s, some firms adopted a sales orientation that encouraged salespeople to aggressively push products on customers. In the 1950s organizations began to adopt a consumer orientation that focused on customer satisfaction and that led to the widespread adoption of the marketing concept. Today, many firms are moving toward a New Era orientation that includes not only a commitment to quality but also concern for both economic and social profit.

3. Marketing decisions cannot be made in isolation from an organization's other operations, so that marketing, finance, manufacturing, research and development, and other functional areas must work together to achieve the organization's goals.

A CASE ANALYSIS EXERCISE

1. Vice president of research and development for the Levi's brand of Levi Strauss & Co.

2. The advertising agency TBWA – Chiat Day.

3. Each of the Levi's brands has specific campaigns targeted to its unique customer base.

4. Goldstein's marketing tasks are multifaceted, and on any given day he might be in brainstorming sessions with the ad agency, attending customer focus groups to determine their shopping habits and media preferences, attending presentations of ideas and sample garments for future seasons, discussing trademark issues regarding use of the Levi's marks around the world, or meeting with retail partners to discuss implementing Levi's marketing programs.

5. The Levi's brand product lines include 501 jeans (the original button-fly model), Red Tab jeans, and Westernwear.

CHAPTER 2

STRATEGIC PLANNING: MAKING CHOICES IN A DYNAMIC ENVIRONMENT

CHAPTER OVERVIEW

In this chapter we learned that strategic planning by top-level managers involves defining the firm's business mission, setting corporate goals and objectives, establishing a business portfolio, and determining its strategic marketing direction. In addition, we considered how decisions about the firm's portfolio of strategic business units are often made with the help of such planning tools as the Boston Consulting Group matrix, and the General Electric/McKinsey business planning grid. Other 'tools' that are used by marketing managers to chart a firm's marketing direction include the product-market growth matrix, and Porter's generic strategy model.

Next we considered how firms gain a competitive advantage when they have distinctive competencies--or capabilities that are stronger than those of the competition.

The marketing planning process determines what strategies and action plans the firm will use to achieve its marketing objectives and the overall strategic goals. Marketing selects the target market(s) the organization will go after and decides what marketing strategies will be used to meet the needs of that market.

Finally, the factors involved in the implementation and control of the marketing plan include the development of a marketing budget, the effective organization of the marketing function, and the establishment of controls in order to measure actual performance and compare with planned performance.

CHAPTER OBJECTIVES

1.   Explain the strategic planning process.

2.   Tell how firms gain a competitive advantage and describe the factors that influence marketing objectives.

3.   Describe the steps in the marketing planning process.

4.   Explain the factors involved in the implementation and control of the marketing plan.

CHAPTER OUTLINE

Please refer to your textbook in order to define, list, and/or describe the missing parts of the chapter outline. The page numbers given will help guide you through this learning process.

I. STRATEGIC PLANNING: GUIDING THE BUSINESS
    Strategic Planning _____ *(p.29)*
    Tactical Planning _____ *(p.29)*
    Operational Planning _____ *(p.30)*
    Cross-Functional Planning _____ *(p.30)*
    A. Defining the Organization's Business Mission _____
        _____ *(p.30)*
        Mission Statement _____ *(p.31)*
    B. Evaluating the Environment: SWOT Analysis _____ *(p.32)*
        1. Internal Environment _____ *(p.32)*
        2. External Environment _____ *(p.32)*
    C. Setting Organizational Objectives _____
        _____ *(p.33)*
        Objectives _____ *(p.33)*
    D. Planning for Growth _____
        1. Portfolio Analysis: Strategic Business Units
            Strategic Business Units _____
            _____ *(p.33)*
            Business Portfolio _____ *(p.33)*
            Portfolio Analysis _____ *(p.34)*
        2. The Boston Consulting Group Matrix _____
            _____ *(p.34)*
            Stars _____ *(p.34)*
            Cash Cows _____ *(p.35)*
            Question Marks _____ *(p.35)*
            Dogs _____ *(p.35)*
        3. Product-Market Growth Matrix _____ *(p.36)*
            Market Penetration _____ *(p.36)*
            Market Development _____ *(p.36)*
            Product Development _____ *(p.36)*
            Diversification _____ *(p.37)*

II. THE MARKETING PLANNING PROCESS
    A. Creating a Competitive Advantage: Marketing's
        Strategic Focus
        Competitive Advantage _____ *(p.39)*
        1. Identifying Distinctive Competencies
            Distinctive Competency _____ *(p.40)*
        2. Providing Differential Benefits
            Differential Benefits _____ *(p.40)*
    B. Setting Marketing Objectives
        1. Sales Objectives _____ *(p.41)*
        2. Product-Oriented Objectives _____ *(p.41)*
        3. Market Objectives _____ *(p.42)*

III. DEVELOPING MARKETING STRATEGIES: ELEMENTS OF A MARKET PLAN
    A.   Selecting a Target Market_____
          _____ *(p.42)*

    B.   Developing Marketing Mix Programs_____
          _____ *(p.43)*
          1.   Product Strategies_____ *(p.43)*
          2.   Pricing Strategies_____ *(p.43)*
          3.   Promotion Strategies_____ *(p.44)*
          4.   Distribution Strategies_____ *(p.44)*

    C.   Preparing a Marketing Plan_____
          _____ *(p.46)*
          Situation Analysis_____ *(p.46)*

IV. IMPLEMENTATION AND CONTROL OF THE MARKETING PLAN
    A.   Implementing the Marketing Plan_____
          _____ *(p.47)*
          1.   The Marketing Budget_____ *(p.47)*
          2.   Organizing the Marketing Function_____
                _____ *(p.48)*
    B.   Controlling the Marketing Plan_____
          _____ *(p.48)*
          1.   Trend Analysis_____ *(p.48)*
          2.   Marketing Research_____ *(p.49)*
          3.   The Marketing Audit_____ *(p.50)*

CHAPTER 2
KEY TERMS
Select the correct term for each definition and write it in the space provided.

Market penetration   Portfolio analysis
Control   Operational planning
Mission statement   Distinctive competency
Competitive advantage   Cross-functional planning
Strategic planning   Marketing budget
Market development   Business portfolio
Objectives   Marketing plan
Implementation

1.   Stategc Planning   A managerial decision process that
                              matches an organization's resources and
                              capabilities to its market opportunities
                              for long-term growth and survival. *(p.29)*

2. _Operational_

A decision process that focuses on developing detailed plans for day-to-day activities that carry out an organization's tactical plans. *(p.30)*

3. _Mission Statement_

A formal statement in an organization's strategic plan that describes the overall purpose of the organization and what it intends to achieve in terms of its customers, products, and resources. *(p.31)*

4. _Objectives_

Specific goals, accomplishments, or outcomes that an organization hopes to achieve by a specific time. *(p.33)*

5. _Business Portfolio_

The group of different businesses, products, or brands owned by an organization and characterized by different income-generating and growth capabilities. *(p.33)*

6. _Portfolio Analysis_

A management tool for evaluating a firm's business mix and assessing the potential of an organization's strategic business units. *(p.34)*

7. _Market Penetration_

Growth strategies designed to increase sales of existing products to current customers, non-users, and users of competitive brands in served markets. *(p.36)*

8. _Market Development_

Growth strategies that introduce existing products to new markets. *(p.36)*

9. _Cross functional_

An approach to planning in which managers work together in developing tactical plans for each functional area in the firm, so that each plan considers the objectives of the other areas. *(p.30)*

10. _Competitive Advantage_

An advantage over competitors that an organization gains through its superior capabilities and unique product benefits that provide greater value in the minds of the consumer. *(p.39)*

11. _Distinctive Competency_

A superior capability of a firm in comparison to its direct competitors. *(p.40)*

12. _Marketing Plan_ A document that identifies where the organization is now, where it wants to go, how it plans to get there, and who will be responsible for carrying out each part of the marketing strategy. *(p.46)*

13. _Implementation_ The stage of the strategic management process in which strategies are put into action on a day-to-day basis. *(p.47)*

14. _Marketing Budget_ A statement of the total amount to be spent on the marketing function and the allocation of money or the spending limit for each activity under a marketer's control. *(p.47)*

15. _Control_ Measuring actual performance, comparing it to planned performance, and making necessary changes in plans and implementation. *(p.48)*

MULTIPLE CHOICE
Identify the most correct answer.

1. A decision process that concentrates on developing detailed plans for strategies and tactics for the short term that supports an organization's long-term strategic plan is: *(p.29)*
   a.   strategic planning.
   b.   tactical planning.
   c.   operational planning.
   d.   short-term planning.

2. In the first stage of strategic planning, a firm's top executives: *(p.30)*
   a.   define the mission of the organization.
   b.   translate the firm's business mission into the goals and objectives of the organization.
   c.   analyze the current organizational structure and evaluate strategies and opportunities for growth that are consistent with its mission and objectives.
   d.   none of the above.

3. A statement of business mission usually covers the following basic areas: *(p.31)*
   a.   the customer segment the firm will serve.
   b.   the nature of the benefits the firm will attempt to supply.
   c.   The stage in the value-adding process in which the firm will compete.
   d.   all of the above.

4. Individual units within the firm that operate like separate businesses, with each having its own mission, business and marketing objectives, resources, managers, and competitors are called: *(p.33)*
   a. corporate operating units (COUs).
   b. the firm's competencies.
   c. strategic business units (SBUs).
   d. the firm's benefits.

5. The Boston Consulting Group (BCG) matrix provides a portfolio management strategy in which: *(p.34)*
   a. mature, market-leading products generate cash that is used for investment in new products.
   b. a detailed assessment of the SBU is based on industry attractiveness and company business strengths.
   c. the grid allows a firm to place its strategic business units into nine different categories based on high, medium, and low industry attractiveness and business strengths.
   d. the process focuses on the firm's product mix and determines whether the firm would be better off putting its resources into existing products or trying to grow by developing or acquiring new products.

6. Cash cows are: *(p.35)*
   a. business units with low market shares in fast-growth markets.
   b. business units with a small share of a slow-growth market.
   c. business units having a dominant market share in a low-growth potential market.
   d. business units having a dominant market share in fast-growth markets.

7. Growth strategies that emphasize both new products and new markets are known as: *(p.37)*
   a. product development.
   b. diversification.
   c. market development.
   d. cost leadership.

8. _____ are business units with a dominant market share in high-growth markets. *(p.34)*
   a. Dogs
   b. Question Marks
   c. Cash Cows
   d. Stars

9. Values customers obtain from using, experiencing, or possessing a firm's product that are superior to those of competing products are called: *(p.40)*
   a. distinctive competency.
   b. differential benefits.
   c. comparative advantage.
   d. consumer superiority.

10. The internal environment of an organization includes: *(p.32)*
    a. the uncontrollable elements outside of an organization that may effect its performance either positively or negatively.
    b. everything from consumers to government regulations to competitors to the overall economy.
    c. the controllable elements inside an organization including its people, its facilities, and how it does things that influence the operations of the organization.
    d. all of the above.

11. Once marketing management has identified the firm's strengths and weaknesses, the next step in the planning process is: *(p.41)*
    a. to develop objectives.
    b. to select a target market.
    c. to develop specific strategies.
    d. to prepare a marketing plan.

12. A product strategy: *(p.43)*
    a. includes pricing objectives and states the specific prices to be charged for a product.
    b. determines what design is best for the product, what features it will have, how it will be packaged, and what warranty it will carry.
    c. includes plans for advertising, consumer sales promotion, trade promotions, the sales function, publicity, and point-of purchase materials.
    d. describes how the product will be made available to targeted customers when and where they want it.

13. The implementation sections of a marketing plan contain: *(p.47)*
    a. a marketing budget.
    b. development of specific action plans.
    c. the assignment of major areas of responsibility to individuals or teams.
    d. all of the above.

14. Product development strategies: *(p.36)*
    a. create growth by selling new products in existing markets.
    b. introduce existing products to new markets.
    c. seek to increase sales of existing products to current customers, nonusers, and users of competing brands in served markets.
    d. emphasize both new products and new markets to achieve growth.

15. A functional structure separates marketing into: *(p.48)*
    a. customer needs or usage by geographic region.
    b. a product or brand.
    c. distinct components, such as advertising, sales promotion, sales force management and marketing research.
    d. sales and market share trends.

CHAPTER IN REVIEW - WRITING TO LEARN

1. Describe how a firm gains a competitive advantage.

   _____

   _____

   _____

2. Discuss the role of marketing strategies in planning and the development of the marketing plan.

   _____

   _____

   _____

3. Explain the factors involved in the implementation and control of the marketing plan.

   _____

   _____

   _____

A Case Analysis Exercise

Real People, Real Choices: Meet Frank Cimermancic, Harley-Davidson, Inc.

Reread the Opening Vignette on page 28 of your text and answer the following questions.

1. Describe the position held by Frank Cimermancic at Harley-Davidson, Inc.

2. How did Frank Cimermancic wind up in a marketing leadership position at Harley-Davidson, Inc.?

3. What was/is the primary responsibility of the Director of Business Planning at Harley-Davidson, Inc.?

4. Identify the constantly changing factors that affect a firm in a dynamic environment.

5. What level of the organization is responsible for initiating the strategic planning process?

ANSWERS
CHAPTER OUTLINE

I. STRATEGIC PLANNING: GUIDING THE BUSINESS
    Strategic Planning--A managerial decision process that matches an organization's resources and capabilities to its market opportunities for long-term growth and survival.
    Tactical Planning--A decision process that concentrates on developing detailed plans for strategies and tactics for the short term that support an organization's long-term strategic plan.
    Operational Planning--A decision process that focuses on developing detailed plans for day-to-day activities that carry out an organization's tactical plans.
    Cross-Functional Planning--An approach to tactical planning in which managers work together in developing tactical plans for each functional area in the firm, so that each plan considers the objectives of the other areas.
    A. Defining the Organization's Business Mission--Top management's vision of why the firm exists and how it will differ from other firms is a strategic decision that influences all other planning efforts in the organization.
        Mission Statement--A formal statement in an organization's strategic plan that describes the overall purpose of the organization and what it intends to achieve in terms of its customers, products, and resources.

B.   Evaluating the Environment: SWOT Analysis--An analysis
     of an organization's strengths and weaknesses and the
     opportunities and threats in its external environment.
     1.   Internal Environment--The controllable elements
           inside an organization including its people, its
           facilities, and how it does things that influence
           the operations of the organization.
     2.   External Environment--The uncontrollable elements
           outside of an organization that may affect its
           performance either positively or negatively.
C.   Setting Organizational Objectives--In the next stage of
     the strategic planning process, top management
     translates the firm's business mission into specific
     goals called objectives.
     Objectives--Specific Goals, accomplishments, or outcomes
     that an organization hopes to achieve by a specific time
     frame.

D.   Planning for Growth
     1.   Portfolio Analysis: Strategic Business Units
           Strategic Business Units--Individual units within
           the firm that operate like separate businesses,
           with each having its own mission, business and
           marketing objectives, resources, managers, and
           competitors.
           Business portfolio--The group of different
           businesses, products, or brands owned by an
           organization and characterized by different income-
           generating and growth capabilities.
           Portfolio Analysis--A management tool for
           evaluating a firm's business mix and assessing the
           potential of an organization's strategic business
           units.

     2.   The Boston Consulting Group Matrix--Provides a
           portfolio management strategy in which mature,
           market-leading products generate cash that is used
           for investment in new products.
           Stars--Get all the firm's attention and huge
           investments. Stars are business units with a
           dominant market share in high-growth markets.
           Cash Cows--Business units having a dominant market
           share in a low-growth potential market.
           Question Marks--Business units with low market
           shares in fast-growth markets.
           Dogs--Business units with a small share of a slow-
           growth market.

     3.   Product-Market Growth Matrix--An assessment of the
           growth potential of existing markets and new
           markets.

Market Penetration--Growth strategies designed to increase sales of existing products to current customers, non-users, and users of competitive brands in served markets.

Market Development--Growth strategies that introduce existing products to new markets.

Product Development--Growth strategies that focus on selling new products in served markets.

Diversification--Growth strategies that emphasize both new products and new markets.

II. THE MARKETING PLANNING PROCESS
  A. Creating a Competitive Advantage: Marketing's Strategic Focus
     Competitive Advantage--An advantage over competitors that an organization gains through its superior capabilities and unique product benefits that provide greater value in the minds of consumers.
     1. Identifying Distinctive Competencies
        Distinctive Competency--A superior capability of a firm in comparison to its direct competitors.
     2. Providing Differential Benefits
        Differential Benefits--Values customers obtain from using, experiencing, or possessing a firm's product that are superior to those of competing products.

  B. Setting Marketing Objectives
     1. Sales Objectives--One or more quantitative goals relating to sales.
     2. Product-Oriented Objectives--A growth strategy that focuses on product development.
     3. Market Objectives--Firms that determine that growth can be achieved with new customers using either market development strategies or diversification strategies.

III. DEVELOPING MARKETING STRATEGIES: ELEMENTS OF A MARKET PLAN
  A. Selecting a Target Market--A market segment is selected because of its attractiveness compared to other markets, as well as the firm's belief that its offerings are most suited to winning customers in that market.

  B. Developing Marketing Mix Programs--Identifying how marketing will accomplish its objectives in the firm's target markets.
     1. Product Strategies--Marketers decide which product(s) to market to each segment targeted and what characteristics of the product will provide unique benefits targeted customers want.

2. Pricing Strategies--A pricing strategy includes pricing objectives and states the specific prices to be charged for a product.
3. Promotion Strategies--Includes plans for advertising, consumer sales promotion, trade promotions, the sales function, publicity, and point-of-purchase materials.
4. Distribution Strategies--Describes how the product will be made available to targeted customers when and where they want it.

C. Preparing a Marketing Plan--A document that identifies where the organization is now, where it wants to go, how it plans to get there, and who will be responsible for carrying out each part of the marketing strategy.
Situation Analysis--The first part of a marketing plan that provides a thorough description of the firm's current situation including its internal and external environments.

IV. IMPLEMENTATION AND CONTROL OF THE MARKETING PLAN
A. Implementing the Marketing Plan--The stage of the strategic management process in which strategies are put into action on a day-to-day basis.
1. The Marketing Budget--A statement of the total amount to be spent on the marketing function and the allocation of money or the spending limit for each activity under a marketer's control.
2. Organizing the Marketing Function--A functional structure separates marketing into distinct components, such as advertising, sales promotion, sales force management, and marketing research. A geographic structure is established when firms feel that customer needs differ by geographic region. A product structure may include a number of different brand managers and product group line managers, each of whom is responsible for an entire brand.

B. Controlling the Marketing Plan--Measuring actual performance, comparing it to planned performance, and making necessary changes in plans and implementation.
1. Trend Analysis--An analysis of past industry or company sales data to determine patterns of change that may continue into the future.
2. Marketing Research--The methods used by a firm to obtain feedback on marketing activities.
3. The Marketing Audit--A comprehensive review of a firm's marketing function.

CHAPTER 2
ANSWERS

<table>
<tr><td>

KEY TERMS

1. Strategic planning
2. Operational planning
3. Mission statement
4. Objectives
5. Business portfolio
6. Portfolio analysis
7. Market penetration
8. Market development
9. Cross-functional planning
10. Competitive advantage
11. Distinctive competency
12. Marketing plan
13. Implementation
14. Marketing budget
15. Control

</td><td>

MULTIPLE CHOICE

1. b
2. a
3. d
4. c
5. a
6. c
7. b
8. d
9. b
10. c
11. a
12. b
13. d
14. a
15. c

</td></tr>
</table>

CHAPTER IN REVIEW - WRITING TO LEARN

1. A competitive advantage means that a firm has developed reasons for customers to select its product over all others in the market. A firm gains a competitive advantage when it has distinctive competencies--or capabilities that are stronger than those of the competition--and is able to provide differential benefits--or product benefits that are uniquely different from the competition. Creating a competitive advantage is the strategic focus of an organization's marketing planning process.

2. The marketing planning process determines what strategies and action plans the firm will use to achieve its marketing objectives and its overall strategic goals. Marketing selects the target market(s) the organization will go after and decides what marketing mix strategies that will be used to meet the needs of that market. Product strategies include decisions about products and product characteristics that will appeal to the target market. Pricing strategies state the specific prices to be charged and are influenced both by the cost of the marketing mix elements and targeted customers' willingness to pay. Promotion strategies includes plans for advertising, consumer and trade sales promotion, the sales function, publicity, point of purchase materials, and other marketing communications activities to reach the target market. Distribution strategies outline how the product will be made available to targeted customers when and where they want. The final step in the marketing planning process is the development of a written marketing plan that describes the

firm's current situation, states the marketing objectives, identifies the specific strategies and action plans that will be used, outlines how the plan will be implemented and controlled. It may include contingency plans that are to be used if objectives are not being met by the initial strategies.

3. Implementation or putting the plan into action includes development of that marketing budget, often using a percentage-of-sales or an objective-and-task method. Also essential to successful implementation is effective organization of the marketing function--that is, how the work is broken up into different jobs and assigned to different people. Control is the measurement of actual performance and comparison with planned performance. Planners may use trend analyses or other forms of marketing research to obtain performance feedback. A comprehensive review of the marketing system is sometimes conducted using a marketing audit.

A CASE ANALYSIS EXERCISE

1. As Director of Business Planning for Harley-Davidson, Mr. Cimcermancic's job is to understand the desires of hard-core bikers, weekend bikers, and biker wanna-bees.

2. Upon graduation from Marquette University in 1973, he decided against an accounting career after discovering that he preferred to work in a field like marketing that permitted a bit more creativity.

3. In this capacity he must constantly peer down the highway, trying to determine what the road will look like in the future and tailor Harley's strategy to stay in the lead in the race for market success.

4. All firms operate in a dynamic environment where, among other factors, consumer interests, new technologies, the competition, and the economy are continuously changing.

5. Strategic planning starts at the very top of the organization, where the firm's executive officers define what the organization is all about and what it wants to achieve.

CHAPTER 3

DECISION MAKING IN THE NEW ERA OF MARKETING: ENRICHING THE MARKETING ENVIRONMENT

CHAPTER OVERVIEW

In this chapter we learned that firms in the New Era of Marketing emphasize social profit as well as economic profit. Companies behave ethically because it is morally right and because it allows them to earn goodwill that helps them achieve economic goals.

Social responsibility means that New Era firms act in ways that benefit the public, the community, and the natural environment. New Era firms also practice social responsibility by promoting cultural diversity--that is, by including people of different sexes, races, ethnic groups, and religions as customers, suppliers, employees, and distribution channel members.

We then considered how Quality-focused firms in the New Era of marketing strive to provide goods and services that go beyond customer expectations about the relationship between cost and value. Total quality management (TQM) is a management philosophy that focuses on satisfying the customer and reducing production costs through such programs as continuous quality improvement, employee empowerment, and a team approach that involves employees in all levels of the organization in cross-functional planning and task-related activities.

Next, we learned about the importance of an organization's internal environment. Success in the New Era of marketing rests heavily on an organization's corporate culture, the set of shared values, attitudes, beliefs that influence its decisions and practices. Another aspect of the internal environment in New Era firms is the value placed on the firm's relationship with its suppliers, intermediaries, competitors, and various publics.

Finally, we reviewed why marketers scan the components of an organization's external business environment. Specifically we considered how important understanding the economic environment, competitive environment, natural environment, technological environment, legal environment, and the sociocultural environment should be to marketing planning.

CHAPTER OBJECTIVES

1. Explain why organizations have adopted a New Era marketing orientation focus on ethics and social responsibility.

2. Describe the New Era emphasis on quality.

3. Discuss some of the important aspects of an organization's internal environment.

4. Explain why marketers scan an organization's external business environment.

CHAPTER OUTLINE

Please refer to your textbook in order to define, list, and/or describe the missing parts of the chapter outline. The page numbers given will help guide you through this learning process.

I. WELCOME TO THE NEW ERA OF MARKETING _____
    _____ *(p.57)*
    Social Profit_____ *(p.57)*
    A. Ethical Behavior in the Marketplace
        Business Ethics_____ *(p.58)*
        1. Code of Ethics_____ *(p.58)*
        2. The High Costs of Unethical Marketplace ____
            Behavior_____ *(p.59)*
        3. Consumerism: Fighting Back
            Consumerism_____ *(p.61)*
            Consumer Bill of Rights_____ *(p.61)*
    B. Ethics in the Marketing Mix_____
        _____ *(p.62)*
        1. Making a Product Safe_____ *(p.62)*
        2. Pricing the Product Fairly_____ *(p.62)*
        3. Promoting the Product Ethically_____
            _____ *(p.63)*
            Puffery_____ *(p.63)*
            Corrective Advertising_____ *(p.63)*
        4. Getting the Product Where It Belongs_____
            _____ *(p.63)*

    C. Social Responsibility: Serving the Environment____
        _____ *(p.63)*
        Environmental Stewardship_____ *(p.63)*
        1. Green Marketing_____ *(p.64)*

    D. Serving Society: Cause Marketing_____
        _____ *(p.65)*

    E. Serving the Community: Promoting Cultural Diversity____
        _____ *(p.66)*

II. DOING IT WELL: A FOCUS ON QUALITY_____
    _____ *(p.67)*
    A. Total Quality Management_____
        _____ *(p.67)*
        1. ISO 9000_____ *(p.68)*
        2. Adding a Dose of Quality to the Marketing Mix____
            _____ *(p.68)*

30

III. THE INTERNAL BUSINESS ENVIRONMENT/CORPORATE RESOURCES AND COMPETENCIES
    A.   Corporate Culture _____ (p.69)
        1.   Risk-Taking Cultures _____ (p.70)
        2.   Profit-Centered Versus People-Centered Cultures ____
              _____ (p.70)

    B.   Relationships with Publics _____ (p.70)
        Publics _____ (p.70)
        1.   Relationships with Suppliers _____ (p.70)
        2.   Relationships with Intermediaries_____ (p.70)
        3.   Relationships with Competitors_____ (p.70)
        4.   Relationships with the Public_____ (p.71)

IV.   SCANNING THE EXTERNAL BUSINESS ENVIRONMENT _____
    _____ (p.71)
    A.   The Economic Environment_____ (p.71)
        1.   The Business Cycle: What Goes Around,
            Comes Around _____ (p.71)
        2.   The Power of Expectations_____ (p.72)
        Consumer Confidence_____ (p.72)

    B.   The Competitive Environment_____ (p.72)
        1.   Analyzing the Competition _____ (p.72)
        Competitive Intelligence_____ (p.73)
        2.   Competition in the Micro Environment
        Discretionary Income_____ (p.73)
        Product Competition_____ (p.73)
        Brand Competition_____ (p.73)
        3.   Competition in the Macro Environment
        Monopoly_____ (p.73)
        Perfect Competition_____ (p.74)
        Oligopoly_____ (p.74)
        Monopolistic Competition_____ (p.74)

    C.   The Technological Environment_____
    _____ (p.75)
        1.   Patent _____ (p.75)

    D.   The Legal Environment_____ (p.75)
        1.   The Watchdogs of Business: Regulatory Agencies____
            _____ (p.75)
        2.   Adapting to a Regulatory Environment_____
            _____ (p.75)
        3.   Navigating the Global Legal Environment_____
            _____ (p.75)

    E.   The Sociocultural Environment_____
    _____ (p.77)
        1.   Demographics_____ (p.77)

CHAPTER 3

KEY TERMS
Select the correct term for each definition and write it in the space provided.

Social responsibility
Corporate culture
Business cycle
Cause marketing
Social profit
Monopoly
Cultural diversity
Business ethics

Total quality management (TQM)
Consumer confidence
Demographics
Consumerism
Quality
Patent
Consumer Bill of Rights

1. _Social Profit_   The benefit an organization and society receive from its ethical practices, community service, efforts to promote cultural diversity, and concern for the natural environment. *(p.57)*

2. _Business ethics_   Rules of conduct for an organization that are standards against which most people in its environment judge what is right and what is wrong. *(p.58)*

3. _Consumerism_   A social movement directed toward protecting consumers from harmful business practices. *(p.61)*

4. _Consumer Bill of Rights_   The rights of consumers to be protected by the federal government, as outlined by President John F. Kennedy, including the right to safety, the right to be heard, the right to be informed, and the right to choose. *(p.61)*

5. _Social Responsibility_   A management practice in which organizations seek to engage in activities that have a positive effect on society and promote the public good. *(p.63)*

6. _Cause Marketing_   A marketing strategy in which an organization seeks to serve its community by promoting and supporting a worthy cause or by allying itself with non-profit organizations to tackle a social problem. *(p.65)*

7. _Cultural Diversity_ — A management practice that emphasizes people of different sexes, races, ethnic groups, and religions in activities involving an organization's employees, customers, suppliers, and distribution channel partners. (p.66)

8. _Quality_ — The level of performance, dependability, and cost that customers expect in products that satisfy their needs and wants. (p.67)

9. _TQM_ — A management philosophy that focuses on satisfying customers though empowering employees to be an active part of continuous quality improvement. (p.67)

10. _Corporat Culture_ — The set of values, norms, beliefs, and practices held by an organization's managers. (p.69)

11. _Patent_ — Legal documentation granting an individual or firm exclusive right to produce and sell a particular invention. (p.75)

12. _Business Cycle_ — The overall patterns of change in the economy--including periods of prosperity, recession, depression, and recovery--that affect consumer and business purchasing power. (p.71)

13. _Consumer Confidence_ — An indicator of future spending patterns as measured by the extent to which people are optimistic or pessimistic about the state of the economy. (p.72)

14. _Monopoly_ — A market situation in which one firm, the only supplier of a particular product, is able to control the price, quality, and supply of that product. (p.73)

15. _Demographic_ — Statistics that measure observable aspects of a population, including size, age, gender, ethnic group, income, education, occupation, and family structure. (p.77)

MULTIPLE CHOICE
Identify the most correct answer.

1. Business ethics is where: *(p.58)*
   a. the firm takes its first step toward creating social profit.
   b. consumer interests are least important.
   c. the marketers' interests are in the forefront.
   d. all of the above.

2. When a consumer purchases an item of clothing such as a party dress or an expensive business suit, wears it for a special occasion, and returns it the next day as if it had not been worn, this is called: *(p.61)*
   a. consumer sovereignty.
   b. rebate scamming.
   c. caveat emptor syndrome.
   d. retailing borrowing.

3. A pricing strategy that is unethical but not illegal is: *(p.60)*
   a. price discrimination strategy.
   b. disclosing the full price associated with any purchase.
   c. price-fixing.
   d. none of the above.

4. Slotting allowances are: *(p.63)*
   a. fees paid by casinos in Las Vegas for marketing slot machines.
   b. lower prices charged by a manufacturer to larger customers.
   c. fees many large retailers are forcing manufacturers to pay for agreeing to stock the company's products on valuable shelf space.
   d. price increases of popular products.

5. Environmental stewardship is: *(p.63)*
   a. a management practice in which organizations seek to engage in activities that have a positive effect on society and promote the public good.
   b. a position taken by an organization to protect or enhance the natural environment as it conducts its business activities.
   c. a social movement directed towards protecting consumers from harmful environmental factors.
   d. the development of the Environmental Bill of Rights.

6. A marketing strategy that supports environmental stewardship by creating an environmentally founded differential benefit in the minds of consumers is called: *(p.64)*
    a. green marketing.
    b. cause marketing.
    c. environmental diversity.
    d. social responsibility.

7. Social profit is: *(p.57)*
    a. a firm's success in achieving dollar profit.
    b. the income statement that shows the economic bottom line of a firm.
    c. the net benefit both the firm and society receive from a firm's ethical practices.
    d. how the firm's profit impacts society.

8. The world's most-admired, successful companies share the following common characteristic(s): *(p.58)*
    a. high quality products or services.
    b. ability to attract and keep talented people.
    c. responsibility to the community and environment.
    d. all of the above.

9. The TQM practice that gives all employees the authority to make decisions about their work without supervisory approval is called: *(p.67)*
    a. Kaizen.
    b. involving all employees.
    c. participatory management program.
    d. relationship marketing.

10. The International Standards Organization: *(p.68)*
    a. is an organization that initially developed a set of criteria in 1987 to regulate product quality in the United States.
    b. is an organization that tests and approves the design and manufacturing .processes to assure the safety of the products.
    c. developed a broad set of guidelines, known as ISO 9000, to cover issues related to the manufacture and installation of products, as well as post-sale servicing.
    d. all of the above.

11. Groups of people--including customers, employees, shareholders, financial institutions, government, the media, and public interest groups--that have interest in an organization are called: *(p.70)*
    a. publics.
    b. business partners.
    c. intermediaries.
    d. activists.

12. The Business Cycle: *(p.71)*
    a. is both a measure of the current state of the economy and a predictor of future economic trends.
    b. represents the total value of goods and services produced in a country regardless of whether the firms are U.S.-or foreign-owned.
    c. grows at about 3 percent per year in the United States.
    d. includes prosperity, recovery, recession, and depression.

13. A marketing situation in which competitors offering very different products compete to satisfy the same consumer needs and wants is known as: *(p.73)*
    a. brand competition.
    b. product competition.
    c. discretionary competition.
    d. consumer competition.

14. A market structure in which a relatively small number of sellers, each holding a substantial share of the market, compete in a market with many buyers is a(n): *(p.74)*
    a. perfect competition.
    b. monopolistic competition.
    c. oligopoly.
    d. adversarial competition.

15. The Federal Trade Commission (FTC): *(p.75)*
    a. enforces laws relating to several areas of business practice including laws against deceptive advertising and product labeling regulations.
    b. regulates bus, truck, rail, and water operations.
    c. protects the public from potentially hazardous materials.
    d. enforces laws and regulations relating to foods, drugs, cosmetics, and veterinary products.

CHAPTER IN REVIEW - WRITING TO LEARN

1. Explain why New Era organizations focus on ethics and social responsibility.

_____

_____

_____

2. Describe the New Era emphasis on quality.

_____

_____

_____

3. Discuss some of the important aspects of an organization's internal environment.

_____

_____

_____

A Case Analysis Exercise

Real People, Real Choices: Meet Joyce LaValle, Interface Americas

Reread the Opening Vignette on page -57 of your text and answer the following questions.

1. What is a Chief Innovations Officer?

2. What is it that Interface Americas produces?

3. While serving in the role as regional vice-president, what are Joyce's responsibilities?

4. How did Interface Americas become a leader in adopting its global ecological approach to business?

5. What is the global scope of manufacturing sites at Interface Americas?

ANSWERS
CHAPTER OUTLINE

I. WELCOME TO THE NEW ERA OF MARKETING
New Era marketers have come to realize that decisions and strategies designed to satisfy consumer needs and wants must not only be economically sound--they must also have a strong ethical foundation and be socially responsible as well.
Social Profit--The benefit an organization and society receive from its ethical practices, community service, efforts to promote cultural diversity, and concern for the natural environment.
   A. Ethical Behavior in the Marketplace
      Business Ethics--Rules of conduct for an organization that are standards against which most people in its environments judge what is right and what is wrong.
      1. Code of Ethics--Written standards of behavior to which everyone in the organization must subscribe.
      2. The High Costs of Unethical Marketplace Behavior--In the New Era of marketing, managers understand that ethical behavior is not only the right way to act, it also serves the best interests of the organization.
      3. Consumerism: Fighting Back

Consumerism--A social movement directed toward protecting consumers from harmful business practices.

Consumer Bill of Rights--The rights of consumers to be protected by the Federal government, as outlined by President John F. Kennedy, including the right to safety, the right to be informed, the right to be heard and the right to choose.

B. The Role of Ethics in the Marketing Mix--New Era Managers also take into account the ethical side of each of the 4 P's in the marketing mix.

1. Making a Product Safe--In developing product strategies, marketing management's key ethical decisions relate to product safety.

2. Pricing the Product Fairly--Many pricing practices are now illegal (price-fixing, and price discrimination).

3. Promoting the Product Ethically--To protect consumers from being misled, the Federal Trade Commission (FTC) has specific regulations regarding unfair or deceptive advertising.

    Puffery--Claims made in advertising of product superiority that cannot be proven true or untrue.

    Corrective Advertising--Advertising that clarifies or qualifies previous deceptive advertising claims.

4. Getting the Product Where It Belongs--The way a firm chooses to get its products to the place where consumers want them at the time they want them can also involve ethical decisions.

C. Social Responsibility: Serving the Environment--A management practice in which organizations seek to engage in activities that have a positive effect on society and promote the public good.

    Environmental Stewardship--A position taken by an organization to protect or enhance the natural environment as it conducts its business activities.

1. Green Marketing--A marketing strategy that supports environmental stewardship by creating an environmentally founded differential benefit in the minds of consumers.

D. Serving Society: Cause Marketing--A marketing strategy in which an organization seeks to serve its community by promoting and supporting a worthy cause or by allying itself with non-profit organizations to tackle a social problem.

E. Serving the Community: Promoting Cultural Diversity--A management practice that emphasizes people of different sexes, races, ethnic groups, and religions in activities involving an organization's employees, customers, suppliers, and distribution channel partners.

II. DOING IT WELL: A FOCUS ON QUALITY--The level of performance, dependability, and cost that customers expect in products that satisfy their needs and wants.
   A. Total Quality Management--A management philosophy that focuses on satisfying customers through empowering employees to be an active part of continuous quality improvement.
      1. ISO 9000--Criteria developed by the International Standards Organization to regulate product quality in Europe.
      2. Adding a Dose of Quality to the Marketing Mix--New Era firms continually seek ways to improve product, place, price, and promotion.

III. THE INTERNAL BUSINESS ENVIRONMENT/CORPORATE RESOURCES AND COMPETENCIES
   A. Corporate Culture--The set of values, norms, beliefs that influence the behavior of everyone in the organization.
      1. Risk-Taking Cultures--Firms that value innovativeness, individuality, and creativity.
      2. Profit-Centered Versus People-Centered Cultures--In New Era firms, where the business mission includes a concern for employees, customers, and society, as well as shareholder profits.

   B. Relationships With Publics--A measure of a firm's internal strengths relates to the relationships it develops outside the organization.
      Publics--Groups of people--including customers, employees, shareholders, financial institutions, government, the media and public interest groups--that have an interest in an organization.
      1. Relationships with Suppliers--New Era firms know that they can't make quality products if they can't get quality parts from their suppliers.
      2. Relationships with Intermediaries--The firms that work with the organization to promote and distribute its goods and services to customers.
      3. Relationships with Competitors--Firms often find it is to their advantage to cooperate with others in the same business.
      4. Relationships with the Public--Companies need to be sensitive to the concerns of various citizens' groups.

IV. SCANNING THE EXTERNAL BUSINESS ENVIRONMENT--Firm's scan the external business environment searching for factors beyond their direct control that create opportunities and pose threats.
   A. The Economic Environment--This means evaluating factors that influence buying patterns.

1. The Business Cycle: What Goes Around, Comes Around-- The overall patterns of change in the economy-- including periods of prosperity, recession, depression, and recovery--that affect consumer and business purchasing power.
2. The Power of Expectations--Many economists suggest that changes in the economy are primarily a "self-fulfilling prophecy."
   Consumer Confidence--An indicator of future spending patterns as measured by the extent to which people are optimistic or pessimistic about the state of the economy.

B. The Competitive Environment--Successful firms take home the gold by taking the lead and keeping ahead of the competition.
   1. Analyzing the Competition--Before a firm can begin to develop strategies that will create a competitive advantage in the marketplace, it has to know who its competitors are and what they're doing.
      Competitive Intelligence--The process of gathering and analyzing publicly available information about rivals.
   2. Competition in the Micro Environment
      Discretionary Income--The portion of income people have left over after paying for necessities such as housing, utilities, food, and clothing.
      Product Competition--When firms offering different products compete to satisfy the same consumer needs and wants.
      Brand Competition--A marketing situation in which firms offering similar products or services, compete for consumers based on their brand's reputation or perceived benefits.
   3. Competition in the Macro Environment
      Monopoly--A market situation in which one firm, the only supplier of a particular product, is able to control the price, quality, and supply of that product.
      Perfect Competition--A market structure in which many small sellers, all of whom offer similar products, are unable to control the quality, price, or supply of a product.
      Oligopoly--A market structure in which a relatively small number of sellers, each holding a substantial share of the market, compete in a market with many buyers.
      Monopolistic Competition--A market structure in which many firms, each having slightly different products, compete in a market with many buyers by offering consumers unique benefits that could allow one firm to monopolize the market.

C.   The Technological Environment--Technological developments that impact marketers today involve the improved abilities of organizations to communicate with customers, complete transactions more effectively, and deliver goods and services more efficiently.
   1.   Patent--Legal documentation granting an individual or firm exclusive right to produce and sell a particular invention.

D.   The Legal Environment--Legal and regulatory controls are prime motivators for many business decisions.
   1.   The Watchdogs of Business: Regulatory Agencies-- Federal and state governments have also created a host of regulatory agencies, to monitor business activities and enforce laws.
   2.   Adapting to a Regulatory Environment--New Era firms know that the best of all worlds is when no government regulation is needed because firms work together to make sure everyone plays fair.
   3.   Navigating the Global Legal Environment--Operating in global markets is difficult because of the variety of regulations that govern business activities in different countries.

E.   The Sociocultural Environment--In both consumer and business-to-business markets, an understanding of social and cultural factors is a must.
   1.   Demographics--Statistics that measure observable aspects of a population, including size, age, gender ethnic group, income, education, occupation, and family structure.

CHAPTER 3
ANSWERS

KEY TERMS

1.   Social profit
2.   Business ethics
3.   Consumerism
4.   Consumer Bill of Rights
5.   Social responsibility
6.   Cause marketing
7.   Cultural diversity
8.   Quality
9.   Total quality management (TQM)
10.   Corporate culture
11.   Entrepreneur
12.   Business cycle
13.   Consumer confidence
14.   Monopoly
15.   Demographics

MULTIPLE CHOICE

1.   a
2.   d
3.   b
4.   c
5.   b
6.   a
7.   c
8.   d
9.   b
10.   c
11.   a
12.   d
13.   b
14.   c
15.   a

CHAPTER IN REVIEW - WRITING TO LEARN

1. Firms in the New Era of Marketing emphasize social profit as well as economic profit. Companies behave ethically because it is morally right and because it allows them to earn good will that helps them achieve economic goals. New Era marketers consider ethical issues in developing marketing strategies and are often influenced by consumerism, a social movement aimed at protecting consumers from harmful business practices.

    Social responsibility means that New Era firms act in ways that benefit the public, the community, and the natural environment. New Era marketers assume social responsibility through environmental stewardship, in which the firm's actions either improve or do not harm the natural environment, and cause marketing, which focus on market strategies that promote the public good.

2. Quality-focused firms in the New Era of marketing strive to provide goods and services that go beyond customer expectations about the relationship between cost and value. Total quality management (TQM) is a management philosophy that focuses on satisfying customers and reducing production costs through such programs a continuous quality improvement, employee empowerment, and a team approach that involves employees in all levels of the organization in crossfunctional planning and task-related activities.

3. Success in the New Era of marketing rests heavily on an organization's corporate culture, the set of shared values, attitudes, beliefs that influence its decisions and practices. New Era firms are more people centered and concerned with the welfare of employees. Another aspect of the internal environment in New Era firms is the value placed on the firm's relationships with its suppliers, intermediaries, competitors, and various publics. Important publics include employees, shareholders, government, media, financial institutions, and consumers.

A CASE ANALYSIS EXERCISE

1. In this role, one is responsible for the marketing, environmental and education initiatives of the company.

2. Interface Americas produces carpet, fabrics, and other interior finishes for the commercial market.

3. Joyce LaValle is responsible for managing sales and marketing organizations for a five-state region.

4. Joyce LaValle was the driving force behind a comprehensive revitalization of the Prince Street division, including the construction of an energy-efficient, earth-friendly production facility in Cartersville, Georgia.

5. Interface Americas has 26 manufacturing sites in the U.S., Canada, the United Kingdom, Holland, Australia, and Thailand.

CHAPTER 4

THINK GLOBALLY AND ACT LOCALLY: MARKETING IN A
MULTINATIONAL ENVIRONMENT

CHAPTER OVERVIEW

Global marketing opportunities can represent a challenging and vast
new frontier. We have discovered that firms choose to enter foreign
markets for several reasons. However, the global game is not always
easy to play: Competition comes from both local and foreign firms,
and differences in national laws, customs, and consumer preferences
can increase the difficulty for any business firm to achieve
success.

A country's stage of economic development determines a global firm's
marketing opportunities. In less developed countries with
subsistence economies, opportunities are usually limited staples and
inexpensive discretionary items. In developing countries, such as
those in Eastern Europe, Latin America, and the Pacific Rim, an
industrial-based economy is evolving and the rising middle class
creates great demand for basic consumer goods. Developed countries
such as Japan have highly sophisticated marketing systems and offer
almost limitless marketing opportunities for goods and services.

We then discussed how elements of the political, legal, and cultural
environments influence a firm's decision to enter global markets.
In some countries but not all, the strong appeal of American
products makes it easy for U.S. firms to go global.

Finally, we considered the different strategies a firm can choose in
order to enter global markets. Specifically we discussed exporting,
licensing, franchising, partnerships or strategic alliances, and
mergers. Sometimes a firm might also evaluate the arguments for a
standardization versus a localization of marketing strategies.

CHAPTER OBJECTIVES

1.   Explain how complex relationships among firms, countries, and
     regions influence world trade.

2.   Understand how political, legal, and cultural issues influence
     global marketing strategies and outcomes.

3.   Explain the strategies a firm can use to enter global markets.

4.   Understand the arguments for standardization versus
     localization of marketing strategies in global markets, and
     understand how elements of the marketing mix apply in foreign
     countries.

CHAPTER OUTLINE

Please refer to your textbook in order to define, list, and/or describe the missing parts of the chapter outline. The page numbers given will help guide you through this learning process.

I. LET'S GET SMALL _____
    _____ (p.85)
    A. World Trade _____ (p.87)
        1. How "Worldly" Can A Company Be?
            Domestic Firm _____ (p.88)
            Exporting Firm _____ (p.88)
            Multinational Firm _____ (p.88)
            Global Firm _____ (p.88)
        2. Countertrade _____ (p.89)
        3. Trade Flow _____ (p.89)

    B. Competitive Advantage _____
        _____ (p.89)
        1. Demand Conditions _____
            _____ (p.89)
        2. Related and Supporting Industries _____
            _____ (p.89)
        3. Factor Conditions _____
            _____ (p.89)
        4. Company Strategy, Structure, and Rivalry _____
            _____ (p.90)

    C. Borders, Roadblocks, and Communities
        1. Protected Trade
            Protectionism _____ (p.90)
            Import Quotas _____ (p.90)
            Embargo _____ (p.90)
            Tariffs _____ (p.90)
            General Agreement on Tariffs and Trade (GATT) ____
            _____ (p.90)
            World Trade Organization (WTO)_____
            _____ (p.90)
        2. Economic Communities _____
            _____ (p.91)
            European Union (EU) _____ (p.91)
            North American Free Trade Agreement (NAFTA)___
            _____ (p.91)

II. THE GLOBAL MARKETING ENVIRONMENT_____
     _____ (p.92)
     A. The Economic Environment_____
         _____ (p.92)
         1. Indicators of Economic Health
             Standard of Living _____ (p.92)
             Gross Domestic Product _____ (p.92)
             Economic Infrastructure _____ (p.92)

45

2.   Level of Economic Development
     Less Developed Country _____ (p.92)
     Developing Countries _____ (p.93)
     Developed Country _____ (p.93)

B.   The Political and Legal Environment _____ (p.94)
     1.   Political Issues
          Economic Sanctions _____ (p.94)
          Nationalization_____ (p.94)
          Expropriation _____ (p.94)
     2.   Regulatory Issues
          Local Content Rules _____ (p.95)
     3.   Human Rights Issues _____ (p.95)

C.   The Cultural Environment_____ (p.96)
     1.   Values
          Cultural Values _____ (p.96)
          Collectivist Culture _____ (p.96)
          Individualist Culture _____ (p.96)
     2.   Norms and Customs
          Norms _____ (p.97)
          Custom _____ (p.97)
          More _____ (p.97)
          Conventions _____ (p.97)
     3.   Symbols and Superstitions
          Semiotics _____ (p.98)
     4.   Language _____ (p.99)
     5.   Ethnocentricity
          Ethnocentrism _____ (p.100)

III. HOW "GLOBAL" SHOULD A MARKETING STRATEGY BE?
     _____ (p.102)
     A.   Company-Level Decisions: Choosing a
          Market Entry Strategy _____ (p.102)
          1.   Exporting
               Export Merchant _____ (p.102)
          2.   Contractual Agreements
               Licensing _____ (p.103)
               Franchising _____ (p.103)
          3.   Strategic Alliances _____ (p.103)
               Joint Venture _____ (p.103)
          4.   Direct Investment _____ (p.105)

     B.   Product-Level Decisions: Choosing a Marketing
          Mix Strategy _____ (p.105)
          1.   Standardization versus Location _____
               _____ (p.106)
          2.   Product Decisions _____ (p.106)
          3.   Promotion Decisions _____ (p.108)
          4.   Price Decisions _____ (p.108)
               Gray Market_____ (p.110)

Dumping _____ (p.110)
5.   Distribution Decisions _____ (p.110)

CHAPTER 4

KEY TERMS
Select the correct term for each definition and write it in the space provided.

Protectionism   Developing country
Economic communities   Joint venture
Standardization   Export merchants
Trade flow   Nationalization
Franchising   Licensing
General Agreement of Tariffs & Trade (GATT)   Competitive advantage
Demand conditions   Political risk
Strategic alliance   assessment

1.   *Trade Flow*   The pattern of economic interdependence among countries or regions. *(p.89)*

2.   *Competitive Advantage*   The superiority of one country in producing certain products due to its resources, technology, or some other factor that gives it an advantage over other countries. *(p.89)*

3.   *Demand Conditions*   A market condition in which a country's (or market's) population growth rate, economic condition, and other characteristics create high levels of demand and potential opportunities for businesses. *(p.89)*

4.   *Developing Country*   A country at the middle stage of economic development, characterized by rising standards of living, some use of technology, a relatively low GDP, a high market potential for many goods, and a potentially attractive labor supply. *(p.93)*

5.   *Economic Comm*   A group of countries who have agreed to work together in the regulation of international trade for the good of all member nations. *(p.91)*

6. _Political risk assessment_   A process in which international marketers weigh a foreign country's market potential against political conditions that may hinder market success. *(p.94)*

7. _Nationalization_   The official seizure of foreign-owned property in a country, without any payment to the foreign owners. *(p.94)*

8. _Protectionism_   Government policies that erect trade barriers in order to protect a country's domestic industries. *(p.90)*

9. _GATT_   A series of agreements the promote international trade among participating countries by reducing taxes and restrictions. *(p.90)*

10. _Export merchants_   Intermediaries in international trade who negotiate sales in foreign countries on behalf of exporting firms for a fee or commission. *(p.102)*

11. _licensing_   A contractual agreement that assigns the limited right to produce and market a firm's goods to another in exchange for a fee or royalties on sales. *(p.103)*

12. _Franchise_   A contractual arrangement that assigns limited rights to an entire business to another in exchange for a fee or royalties on sales. *(p.103)*

13. _Strategic Alliance_   A formal partnership agreement between two firms to pool their resources in order to achieve common goals. *(p.103)*

14. _joint venture_   A strategic equity alliance that usually results in a jointly run corporate entity. *(p.103)*

15. _Standardization_   An international marketing perspective in which the same marketing mix strategies are used in all global markets. *(p.106)*

MULTIPLE CHOICE
Identify the most correct answer.

1. A country at the lowest stage of economic development is categorized as a: *(p.92)*
   a. less developed country (LDC).
   b. subsistence-economy country(SEC).
   c. limited-market country (LMC).
   d. technology-deficient country (TDC).

2. A developed country is characterized by: *(p.93)*
   a. weak private enterprise.
   b. strong private enterprise.
   c. a market potential for limited goods and services.
   d. all of the above.

3. Government actions that prohibit or restrict trade with a particular country for political reasons are: *(p.94)*
   a. strategic alliances.
   b. closed trade zoning.
   c. global prohibition.
   d. economic sanctions.

4. Expropriation is: *(p.94)*
   a. the official seizure of foreign-owned property in a country, without any payment to the foreign owners.
   b. voluntary payments by a foreign owner to get an illegal advantage.
   c. the official seizure of foreign-owned property in a country, frequently without full-value payment to the foreign owners.
   d. payment extracted under duress by someone in authority from a person seeking what they are lawfully entitled to.

5. A government trade regulation limiting the quantity of certain goods is allowed entry into a country is a(n): *(p.90)*
   a. tariff.
   b. quota.
   c. embargo.
   d. dumping.

6. An ad valorem tariff is: *(p.90)*
   a. a tax based on the number of items imported.
   b. a tax regulating advertising of items imported.
   c. a tax based on the value of the product imported.
   d. a tax based on the price advantage of domestic products.

7. Government regulations on the production of goods by foreign manufacturers that control the portion of domestic components used in the manufacturing process are called: *(p.129)*
   a. domestic component laws.
   b. the General Agreement of Tariffs and Trade.
   c. The Generalized System of Preferences.
   d. local content rules.

8. An exporting strategy: *(p.102)*
   a. allows a firm to sell its products in global markets.
   b. cushions the firm against downturns in its domestic market.
   c. allows the firm to maintain control over design and production decisions.
   d. all of the above.

9. A contractual arrangement involving the right to adapt an entire system of doing business. *(p.103)*
   a. franchising.
   b. subcontracting.
   c. insourcing.
   d. joint venturing.

10. Ethnocentrism: *(p.100)*
    a. involves cooperation between two firms who work together on the same task.
    b. the tendency to prefer products or people of one's own culture.
    c. is an agreement between firms that requires cooperation to market a new product.
    d. is also known as outsourcing.

11. An agreement between firms that requires a deeper commitment to a foreign market and a domestic firm in the target country is a: *(p.103)*
    a. strategic alliance.
    b. bilateral financial venture.
    c. financial investment alliance.
    d. strategic horizontal synergy.

12. Guideline(s) for choosing a standardized strategy over a localized strategy include: *(p.106)*
    a. low cost of R&D.
    b. unique cultural factors influencing consumption.
    c. high promotion via universal image.
    d. all of the above.

13. A firm can encounter gray marketing practices in which of the following: *(p.110)*
    a. competing firms agree to coordinate pricing strategies.
    b. other foreign firms in a country deliberately undercut their prices to gain a foothold in the market.
    c. a company tries to get a toehold in a foreign market by pricing its products lower than they are offered at home.
    d. developing countries are allowed to export goods duty-free.

14. A custom with a strong moral overtone. *(p.97)*
    a. culture.
    b. conventions.
    c. norms.
    d. more.

15. An international marketing perspective in which marketing mix strategies are adapted for different global markets is: *(p.106)*
    a. localization.
    b. comparative advantage.
    c. standardization.
    d. global market adaptation.

CHAPTER IN REVIEW - WRITING TO LEARN

1. Explain why firms decide to seek global marketing opportunities.

   _____

   _____

   _____

2. Describe how undeveloped, developing, and developed countries provide different global marketing opportunities.

   _____

   _____

   _____

3. Discuss the arguments for standardization versus localization of marketing strategies.

_____

_____

_____

A Case Analysis Exercise

Real People, Real Choices: Meet Peter Einstein, a Decision-Maker at MTV Europe

Reread the Opening Vignette on page 85 of your text and answer the following questions.

1. Who is Peter Einstein?

2. What are the functions of MTV Europe?

3. Describe Peter Einstein's responsibilities.

4. Where is MTV Europe based?

5. Describe Mr. Einstein's career.

ANSWERS
CHAPTER OUTLINE

I. LET'S GET SMALL--The world is becoming a smaller place, so the smart marketer needs to think globally by setting its sights on diverse markets around the world, but act locally by being willing to adapt its business practices to conditions in other parts of the globe.
   A. World Trade--Many successful firms know that going global is an option they can't ignore.
      1. How "Worldly" Can A Company Be?
         Domestic firm--Confines its sales and marketing efforts to its home market.
         Exporting firm--Expands sales by offering its products for sale in other countries.
         Multinational firm--Operates in many foreign markets, and modifies the product it sells accordingly.
         Global firm--Views the world as its market, and tends to operate the same way in many countries, adapting strategy when necessary to conform to local conditions.
      2. Countertrade--Type of trade in which goods are paid for with other items instead of with cash.

52

3. Trade Flow--The pattern of economic interdependence among countries or regions.

B. Competitive Advantage--A company's success in both domestic and foreign markets depends on conditions in its home country that make it easier or harder to compete.
   1. Demand Conditions--The number and sophistication of domestic customers for a product.
   2. Related and Supporting Industries--Companies must have access to other firms that provide high-quality products and services they require to turn out competitive products.
   3. Factor Conditions--The quality of a country's resources, including its infrastructure, the educational level of its people, and the availability of raw materials.
   4. Company Strategy, Structure, and Rivalry--The way a country's businesses are organized and managed, and the intensity of competition that creates pressure to innovate.

C. Borders, Roadblocks, and Communities
   1. Protected Trade
      Protectionism--Policy adopted by ha government to give domestic companies an advantage.
      Import Quotas--Limitations set by a government on the amount of a product allowed to enter or leave a country.
      Embargo--A quota completely prohibiting specified goods from entering or leaving a country.
      Tariffs--Taxes on imported goods.
      General Agreement on Tariffs and Trade (GATT)--International Treaty to reduce import tax levels and trade restrictions.
      World Trade Organization (WTO)--Formed to mediate trade disputes between nations and to deal with cases in which unfair protectionism by one country is claimed by another.
   2. Economic Communities--Groups of countries that band together to promote trade among themselves and to make it easier for member nations to compete elsewhere.
      European Union (EU)--Economic community that now includes most of Western Europe.
      North American Free Trade Agreement (NAFTA)--The world's largest economic community composed of the United States, Canada, and Mexico.

II. THE GLOBAL MARKETING ENVIRONMENT--How economic, political, and cultural factors affect marketers' global strategies.
   A. The Economic Environment--Countries vary in terms of their economic development.

53

1. Indicators of Economic Health
   Standard of Living—An indicator of the average quality and quantity of goods and services consumed in a country.
   Gross Domestic Product--The total dollar value of goods and services produced by a nation in a year.
   Economic Infrastructure--The quality of a country's distribution, financial, and communications systems.
2. Level of Economic Development
   Less Developed Country--A country that boasts sophisticated marketing systems, strong private enterprise, and bountiful market potential for many goods and services.
   Developing Countries--Countries in which the economy is shifting its emphasis from agriculture to industry.
   Developed Country--A country that boasts sophisticated marketing systems, strong private enterprise, and bountiful market potential for many goods and services.

B. The Political and Legal Environment--When entering a foreign market, a firm must carefully weigh political and legal risks.
   1. Political Issues
      Economic Sanctions--Trade prohibitions imposed by one country against another.
      Nationalization--A domestic government's takeover of a foreign company for its assets with some reimbursement, though often not for the full value.
      Expropriation--A domestic government's seizure of a foreign company's assets without any compensation.
   2. Regulatory Issues
      Local Content Rules--A form of protectionism stipulating that a certain proportion of a product must consist of components supplied by industries in the host country.
   3. Human Rights Issues--Some governments and individual companies are especially vigilant about denying business opportunities to countries that mistreat their citizens.

C. The Cultural Environment--A firm needs to understand and adapt to the customs characteristics, and practices of its citizens.
   1. Values
      Cultural Values--A society's deeply held beliefs about right and wrong ways to live.
      Collectivist Culture--Culture in which people subordinate their personal goals tot hose of a stable community.

Individualist Culture--Culture in which people tend to attach more importance to personal goals than to those of the larger community.
2. Norms and Customs
   Norms--Specific rules dictating what is right or wrong, acceptable or unacceptable.
   Custom--A norm handed down from the past that controls basic behaviors.
   More--A custom with a strong moral overtone.
   Conventions--Norms regarding the conduct of everyday life.
3. Symbols and Superstitions
   Semiotics--Field of study that examines how meanings are assigned to symbols.
4. Language--Language barriers can be big obstacles to marketers breaking into foreign markets.
5. Ethnocentricity
   Ethnocentrism--The tendency to prefer products or people of one's own culture.

III. HOW "GLOBAL" SHOULD A GLOBAL MARKETING STRATEGY BE?--A company must decide on the nature of its commitment, including whether it will partner with another firm or go it alone.
   A. Company Level Decisions--A firm deciding to go global must determine the level of commitment it is willing to make to operate in another country.
      1. Exporting
         Export Merchant--An intermediary used by a firm to represent it in another country
      2. Contractual Agreements
         Licensing--Agreement in which one firm gives another firm the right to produce and market its product in a specified location in return for royalties.
         Franchising--A form of licensing involving the right to adapt an entire system of doing business.
      3. Strategic Alliances--Relationship developed between a firm seeking a deeper commitment to a foreign market and a domestic firm in the target country.
         Joint Venture--Strategic alliance in which a new entity owned by two or more firms is created to allow the partners to pool their resources for common goals.
      4. Direct Investment--When a firm expands internationally, buying a business outright in the host country.
   B. Product-Level Decisions: Choosing a Marketing Mix Strategy--It may or may not be necessary to develop a customized marketing mix for each country.

1. Standardization versus Location--Basic needs and wants are the same everywhere; or, each country has a national character with a distinctive set of behavioral and personality characteristics.
2. Product Decisions--To sell a product in a foreign market there are three choices that include: a straight extension strategy, a product adaptation strategy, and a product invention strategy.
3. Promotion Decisions--It may be necessary to change product promotions in a foreign market.
4. Price Decisions--Costs associated with transportation, tariffs, differences in currency exchange rates, bribes, etc. may affect the price abroad.
   Gray Market---An unauthorized party imports products and then sells them for a fraction of the price.
   Dumping--A company tries to get a toehold in a foreign market by pricing its products lower than they are offered at home.
5. Distribution Decisions--A reliable distribution system is essential if the marketer is to succeed in a foreign market.

CHAPTER 4
ANSWERS

KEY TERMS

1. Trade flow
2. Competitive advantage
3. Demand conditions
4. Developing country
5. Economic communities
6. Political risk assessment
7. Nationalization
8. Protectionism
9. General Agreement of Tariffs & Trade (GATT)
10. Export merchants
11. Licensing
12. Franchising
13. Strategic alliance
14. Joint venture
15. Standardization

MULTIPLE CHOICE

1. a
2. b
3. d
4. c
5. b
6. c
7. d
8. d
9. a
10. b
11. a
12. c
13. b
14. d
15. a

CHAPTER IN REVIEW - WRITING TO LEARN

1. Firms choose to enter foreign markets for several reasons. The principle of comparative advantage means that each country should produce what it is best at. A country's market potential is based on its rate of population growth and economic conditions. A decline in domestic demand for particular products encourages some firms to look at foreign markets for growth.

2. A country's stage of economic development determines a global firm's marketing opportunities. In less developed countries with subsistence economies, opportunities are usually limited to staples and inexpensive discretionary items. In developing countries, such as those in Eastern Europe, Latin America, and the Pacific Rim, an industrial-based economy is evolving and the rising middle class creates great demand for basic consumer goods. Developed countries such as Japan have highly sophisticated marketing systems and offer almost limitless marketing opportunities for goods and services.

3. Firms that operate in two or more countries can choose to standardize their marketing strategies--that is, use the same strategies in all countries--or to localize by adopting different strategies for each market. Proponents of standardization perspective focus on commonalities across countries. Supporters of the localization perspective seek to adapt to the national character of each country.

A CASE ANALYSIS EXERCISE

1. Peter Einstein is the General in charge of MTV's invasion of Europe. As Director of Marketing and Network Development for MTV Europe, he is a key decision-maker in the battle to shape the musical tastes of Europe's youth.

2. MTV Europe is a pan-European cable and satellite channel that transmits music-based programs for young adults across the continent. The network has a single feed across Europe and broadcasts in English.

3. Peter Einstein has overall responsibility for all business areas affecting the growth and development of MTV Networks throughout Europe. He must decide what markets to enter, and help to design the most appealing way for MTV Europe to win the loyalty of viewers in each country, from Switzerland to Spain.

4. Based in London, MTV Europe was the first attempt by American-based MTV Network to bring its music programming to another continent.

5. Mr. Einstein began his fourteen-year career with MTV Networks in the United States where he helped catapult MTV, Nickelodeon, Nick at Nite, and VH-1 into nearly every cable home in America before joining MTV Europe in 1990.

CHAPTER 5

MARKETING INFORMATION AND RESEARCH: ANALYZING THE BUSINESS ENVIRONMENT

CHAPTER OVERVIEW

In reading this chapter we learned that a marketing information system (MIS) is a system for gathering, sorting, analyzing, storing and distributing relevant marketing information. Information included in the MIS often may be primary data that is specifically collected and organized for a particular marketing need and secondary data gathered for some purpose other than the current marketing need.

We also considered the research process that begins with defining the problem to be researched and choosing the type of research that will provide the needed information. Exploratory research may be necessary to identify specific questions or issues, which can be addressed through problem-solving research. Good research methodology will assure data that are reliable, valid, and representative of the population of interest. In addition, we discovered the importance of marketing research to the firm in a global marketplace, where barriers to conducting marketing research may be related to the infrastructure of a country, translation problems, and legal restrictions.

Finally in this chapter we reviewed the variety of research techniques available to marketers (including Exploratory research, Problem-solving research, Causal problem-solving research, and Descriptive research). In addition, the true value of research to the firm will be in how marketers implement the research results.

CHAPTER OBJECTIVES

1. Describe the marketing research process.

2. Understand the differences among exploratory, problem-solving, and causal research, and describe some research techniques available to marketers.

3. Understand the issues involved in making sense of research results.

4. Discuss how marketers implement research results.

CHAPTER OUTLINE

Please refer to your textbook in order to define, list, and/or describe the missing parts of the chapter outline. The page numbers given will help guide you through this learning process.

I.   INFORMATION IS COOL _____
     _____ (p.122)
     Marketing Research _____
     _____ (p.122)
     A.   Information Needs
          1.   Ongoing Information_____
               _____ (p.123)
          2.   Monitored Information_____
               _____ (p.123)
          3.   Specific Information_____
               _____ (p.123)
II. THE STEPS IN MARKETING RESEARCH
     A.   Defining the Problem_____
          _____ (p.125)
          1.   Specifying the Research Objectives _____
               _____ (p.125)
          2.   Identifying the Consumer
               Population of Interest _____ (p.125)
          3.   Placing the Problem in an
               Environmental Context _____ (p.125)
     B.   Determining the Research Technique
          Research Design _____ (p.125)
          1.   Exploratory Research_____
               _____ (p.126)
               Consumer Interviews _____ (p.127)
               Focus Group _____ (p.128)
               Projective Techniques _____
               _____ (p.128)
               Case Study _____ (p.128)
               Ethnography _____ (p.129)
          2.   Descriptive Research _____
               _____ (p.130)
               Cross-Sectional Design _____
               _____ (p.130)
               Longitudinal Design _____
               _____ (p.130)
               Survey _____
               _____ (p.130)
          3.   Causal Research _____
               _____ (p.133)
               Experiments _____ (p.133)
     C.   Gathering Data
          Secondary Data _____
          _____ (p.134)
          Primary Data _____
          _____ (p.134)

60

      1.   Gathering Data in Foreign Countries _____ *(p.135)*

      2.   Searching for the Pot of Gold: Single Source_____
           Data and Data Mining _____
           Single-Source Data _____ *(p.135)*
           Data Mining _____ *(p.136*

D.   Ensuring the Quality of the Research:
    Garbage In, Garbage Out
    1.   Validity _____ *(p.137)*
    2.   Reliability _____ *(p.137)*
    3.   Representativeness _____ *(p.137)*
        Sampling _____ *(p.137)*

E.   Implementing the Research Results _____ *(p.138)*
    1.   Integrating Feedback into Long-Term Planning _____ *(p.139)*
        Marketing Information System (MIS) _____ *(p.139)*
    2.   Predicting the Future _____ *(p.140)*
        Scenarios _____ *(p.140)*

CHAPTER 5

KEY TERMS
Select the correct term for each definition and write it in the space provided.

Validity	Primary data
Marketing research	Representativeness
Research design	Causal research
Survey	Marketing information system (MIS)
Reliability	Exploratory research
Projective techniques	Focus group
Marketing intelligence	Single-source data
Experiment	

1.   ___*MIS*___   An organization's system for continuously gathering, sorting, analyzing, storing, and distributing to managers relevant and timely marketing information. *(p.139)*

2.   ___*MI*___   Information gathered from sources outside the firm about developments in the firm's business environment, including the activities of competitors, that affect the firm. *(p.123)*

3. _Primary Data_ Data specifically collected and organized for a particular marketing information need, or to solve a particular marketing problem. *(p.134)*

4. _Marketing Research_ Systematic and objective collection, analysis, and interpretation of data for use in making informed marketing decisions. *(p.122)*

5. _Single Source_ Data gathered by research services that use technologies to monitor a particular consumer group's exposure to television advertising messages and to track purchases made by the group over time. *(p.135)*

6. _Exploratory_ A type of marketing research designed to investigate or explore a marketing issue or problem that is not well-defined by gathering qualitative descriptive information from a small group of consumers. *(p.126)*

7. _Reliability_ An evaluation criterion that indicates the extent to which marketing research techniques are dependable and consistent and will give the same results time after time. *(p.137)*

8. _Validity_ An evaluation criterion that indicates the extent to which marketing research actually measures what it was intended to measure. *(p.137)*

9. _Representativeness_ An evaluation criterion for marketing research that indicates the extent to which data collected from respondents can be generalized to the larger customer group. *(p.137)*

10. _Design_ The overall research plan that specifies the appropriate research techniques to be used for conducting a research study. *(p.125)*

11. _Focus Group_ An exploratory research technique in which a small group of participants are recruited to join in a discussion of a product, an ad, or some other topic of interest to marketers. *(p.128)*

12. _Projective techniq_   A group of exploratory research techniques that attempt to identify people's underlying feelings by asking them to respond to an ambiguous object, picture, or other stimulus. *(p.128)*

13. _Causal_   A type of problem-solving research that seeks to identify the cause or reason for a marketing phenomenon of interest. *(p.133)*

14. _Experiment_   A research methodology in which pre-specified relationships among variables are tested in a controlled environment. *(p.133)*

15. _Survey_   A descriptive research technique used to collect, summarize, and analyze the responses of a large number of people questioned about a research topic. *(p.130)*

MULTIPLE CHOICE
Identify the most correct answer.

1. Information that is needed to make smart decisions is: *(p.123)*
   a.   ongoing Information.
   b.   monitored Information.
   c.   specific Information.
   d.   all of the above.

2. Data used by marketing, but gathered for some purpose other than a current marketing information need is called: *(p.134)*
   a.   outside data.
   b.   secondary data.
   c.   miscellaneous data.
   d.   primary data.

3. A survey is: *(p.130)*
   a.   a questionnaire asking participants about their beliefs or behaviors.
   b.   published research on the state of the industry conducted by trade organizations.
   c.   data obtained from the Census Bureau.
   d.   all of the above.

4. A research technique used by market researchers that tracks the responses of the same sample of respondents over time is a(n): *(p.130)*
   a. form of descriptive research.
   b. longitudinal design.
   c. cross-sectional design.
   d. customized survey.

5. Defining the problem to be addressed by the research has the following component(s): *(p.125)*
   a. specifying the research objectives.
   b. identifying the consumer population of interest.
   c. placing the problem in an environmental context.
   d. all of the above.

6. Causal research: *(p.133)*
   a. investigates or explores a marketing problem that is not yet well-defined.
   b. provides qualitative data, where the researcher collects data that add "personality and character" to descriptions of consumers' attitudes, feelings, and buying behaviors.
   c. Techniques that attempt to understand cause-and-effect relationships.
   d. is relatively flexible and unstructured to allow researchers to follow-up on each consumer's unique responses in depth.

7. Using whomever is available and willing to participate in the research study is called: *(p.138)*
   a. convenience sampling.
   b. quota sampling
   c. random sampling.
   d. systematic sampling.

8. Sophisticated analysis techniques used by firms to take advantage of the massive amount of transaction information that is now available is known as: *(p.136)*
   a. sugging.
   b. Pot of Gold.
   c. data mining.
   d. search-soliciting.

9. The extent to which research measurement techniques are free from errors is: *(p.137)*
   a. reliability.
   b. validity.
   c. representativeness.
   d. consistency.

10. A product-oriented discussion among a small group of consumers led by a trained moderator is: *(p.128)*
    a. product testing group.
    b. a focus group.
    c. an omnibus survey.
    d. random sampling.

11. Back-translation: *(p.135)*
    a. is a process used by many researchers trying to minimize the problems associated with mistranslation of a language.
    b. requires a questionnaire to be translated into a second language by a native speaker of that language.
    c. requires the new version of the questionnaire to be translated back into the original language.
    d. all of the above.

12. Exploratory research techniques that attempt to identify people's behavior by observing their everyday activities and gathering in-depth qualitative data to understand that behavior are: *(p.127)*
    a. projective techniques.
    b. observational techniques.
    c. behavior techniques.
    d. interviewing techniques.

13. A type of problem-solving research that seeks to describe a specific issue or problem without looking for the reason or cause of the phenomenon is: *(p.130)*
    a. a case study.
    b. field research.
    c. descriptive research.
    d. hypothesizing.

14. This descriptive research technique that relies on nonhuman devices to record behavior is: *(p.131)*
    a. mechanical observation.
    b. cross-sectional design.
    c. a Likert scale.
    d. longitudinal design.

15. Data-collection methods used in descriptive research studies that rely on evidence of people's behavior rather than responses to questions about it are known as: *(p.131)*
    a. personal observation.
    b. unobtrusive measures.
    c. mechanical observation.
    d. all of the above.

1. Discuss some of the issues marketers face when conducting marketing research.

_____

_____

_____

2. Describe the variety of research techniques available to marketers.

_____

_____

_____

3. Discuss how marketers implement the research results.

_____

_____

_____

A Case Analysis Exercise

Real People, Real Choices: Meet Dee Dee Gordon, A Decision Maker at Lambesis

Reread the Opening Vignette on page 122 of your text and answer the following questions.

1. What is the L Report?

2. What is coolhunting?

3. What is the research base of the L Report?

4. How did Dee Dee Gordon become interested in marketing research?

5. What were the origins of the L Report?

ANSWERS
CHAPTER OUTLINE

I. INFORMATION IS COOL--Business firms succeed by knowing what consumers want, when they want it, where they want it—and what competing firms are doing about it.
Marketing Research--The process of collecting, analyzing, and interpreting data about customers, competitors, and the business environment in order to improve marketing effectiveness.

   A. Information Needs
      1. Ongoing Information--Marketing managers use daily or weekly sales data to measure progress toward sales goals and market share objectives.
      2. Monitored Information--Marketing intelligence--Information about a firm's external environment, which allows marketers to monitor conditions that affect demand for existing products or create demand for new products.
      3. Specific Information--Marketing managers use immediate feedback, or specific information to identify opportunities for new products, etc.

II. THE STEPS IN MARKETING RESEARCH
   A. Defining the Problem--Defining the research problem as precisely as possible allows marketers to research for the right answers to the right questions. The three components include:
      1. Specifying the Research Objectives--What questions will the research attempt to answer?
      2. Identifying the Consumer Population of Interest--What are the characteristics of the consumers involved in the problem situation?
      3. Placing the Problem in an Environmental Context--What factors in the firm's internal and external business environment might be influencing the situation?
   B. Determining the Research Technique
   Research Design--A plan that specifies what information will be collected and what type of study will be done.
      1. Exploratory Research--A technique used by marketers to generate insights for future, more rigorous studies.
      Consumer Interviews--One-on-one discussions between a consumer and a researcher.
      Focus Group--A product-oriented discussion among a small group of consumers led by a trained moderator.
      Projective Techniques--Tests used by marketers to explore people's underlying feelings about a product, especially appropriate when consumers are unable or unwilling to express their true reactions.

Case Study--A comprehensive examination of a particular firm or organization.

Ethnography--A detailed report based on observations of people in their own homes or communities.

2. Descriptive Research--A tool used by marketers that probes more systematically into the problem and bases its conclusions on larger numbers of observations.

Cross-Sectional Design--A type of descriptive technique used by marketers that involves the systematic collection of quantitative information.

Longitudinal Design--A technique used by market researchers that tracks the responses of the same sample of respondents over time.

Survey--A questionnaire used by market researchers that asks participants about their beliefs or behaviors. The different types include: Mail, Telephone, Face-to-Face, On-Line, Personal Observation, and Mechanical Observation.

3. Causal Research--Techniques that attempt to understand cause-and-effect relationships.

Experiments--Techniques used by researchers that test prespecified relationships among variables in a controlled environment.

C. Gathering Data

Secondary Data--The purchase of existing data or data which has been collected by other organizations such as the U.S. government's census data.

Primary Data--Collected for the specific purposes of the study.

1. Gathering Data in Foreign Countries--Market conditions and consumer preferences vary widely in different parts of the world, and there are big differences in the sophistication of market research operations and the amount of data available to global marketers.

2. Searching for the Pot of Gold: Single Source Data and Data Mining.

Single-Source Data--Information that is integrated from multiple sources, to monitor the impact of marketing communications on a particular customer group over time.

Data Mining--Sophisticated analysis techniques used by firms to take advantage of the massive amount of transaction information now available. Four important applications include: customer acquisition, customer retention, customer abandonment, market basket analysis.

D. Ensuring the Quality of the Research: Garbage In, Garbage Out
   1. Validity--The extent to which research actually measures what it was intended to measure.
   2. Reliability--The extent to which research measurement techniques are free of errors.
   3. Representativeness--The extent to which consumers in a study are similar to a larger group in which the organization has an interest.
   Sampling--The process of selecting respondents who statistically represent a larger population of interest. Specific techniques include: Random sampling, a quota sample, and a convenience sample.
E. Implementing the Research Results--The preparation of a report of the research results and their integration into long-term planning.
   1. Integrating Feedback into Long-Term Planning--Marketing research is an ongoing process of collecting and interpreting information that should be constantly referred to and updated as the company conducts long-term planning.
   Marketing Information System (MIS)--A technique developed by a firm to continuously gather, sort, analyze, store, and distribute relevant and timely marketing information to its managers.
   2. Predicting the Future--Futurists try to imaging different scenarios, or possible future situations.
   Scenarios---Possible future situations used by futurists to assess likely impact of alternative marketing strategies.

CHAPTER 5
ANSWERS

KEY TERMS		MULTIPLE CHOICE	
1.	Marketing Information System (MIS)	1.	d
2.	Marketing intelligence	2.	b
3.	Primary data	3.	a
4.	Marketing research	4.	b
5.	Single-source data	5.	d
6.	Exploratory research	6.	c
7.	Reliability	7.	a
8.	Validity	8.	c
9.	Representativeness	9.	a
10.	Research design	10.	b
11.	Focus group	11.	d
12.	Projective techniques	12.	b
13.	Causal research	13.	c
14.	Experiment	14.	a
15.	Survey	15.	d

CHAPTER IN REVIEW - WRITING TO LEARN

1. The continued ability of marketing researchers to collect information is strongly tied to ethical research issues including deceptive practices of unscrupulous marketers, privacy issues, and special ethical concerns in conducting research with children. When operating in a global marketplace, barriers to conducting marketing research may be related to the infrastructure of a country, translation problems, and legal restrictions.

2. Exploratory research seeks qualitative data through such techniques as individual interviews, focus groups, projective techniques, and observational techniques such as ethnography. Causal research seeks to identify the cause or reason why something occurs and means designing laboratory or field research experiments which can test pre-specified relationships. Descriptive studies may attempt to describe an issue or problem at one point in time (cross-sectional design) or over time (longitudinal designs).

3. In order for research data to be useful to marketers, it must be sorted, organized and analyzed. How data are handled is influenced by the research methods (exploratory, causal, cross-sectional, longitudinal, and so on), how the data are collected (phone, mail, or personal interview), and the types of questions asked (open-ended versus closed response). Effective marketing managers see research as an ongoing problem-solving process that must be constantly referred to and updated.

A CASE ANALYSIS EXERCISE

1. The L Report is a publication that tracks trends in youth culture.

2. Coolhunting is a research technique that uses input from trendsetting young consumers around the globe to provide forecasts of emerging cool products and styles to clients.

3. The L Report relies on a network of 1,800 young respondents in six U.S. cities to provide up-to-the-minute reports on what's hot and what's not. It also polls kids in Tokyo, London, Amsterdam, Milan, Barcelona, and Sydney to stay on top of global trends.

4. Gordon's interest in marketing research started in the early 1990s, when she opened a clothing boutique in Boston called Placid Planet. Gordon discovered she had a knack for identifying hot new styles, and she began to think about using her skills in other ways.

5.   In 1995 Gordon created a prototype of the L Report and the California-based advertising agency Lambesis decided to publish it four times a year. The L Report provides advice on emerging trends in fashion, sporting events, music, and technology to several Fortune 500 companies.

CHAPTER 6

WHY PEOPLE BUY: CONSUMER BEHAVIOR

CHAPTER OVERVIEW

The purpose of this chapter was to gain a better understanding of what factors influence consumer behavior. Specifically, we considered a number of internal factors that influence consumer behavior including the perception process, and the theories of motivation. In addition, a consumer's attitude is a lasting evaluation of a person, object, or issue. Consumers seek products that are consistent with their attitudes, while marketers often attempt to change these attitudes.

We also reviewed how consumer purchasing decisions and buying behavior are influenced by many factors that include personal, social, and situational issues. The personal influences on consumers are important determinants of their needs and wants. Such factors as age, income, family status, and chosen lifestyle are strongly related to the types of products people buy and the specific brands they want.

The consumer decision-making process includes every activity in the prepurchase, purchase, and postpurchase stages of the process. The degree to which consumers commit themselves to the decision process is determined by the perceived risks associated with the purchase and the relative importance of the perceived consequences to the consumer.

CHAPTER OBJECTIVES

1.   Explain why understanding consumer behavior is important to organizations.

2.   Describe how internal factors influence consumer's decision making processes.

3.   Understand how situational factors can influence consumer behavior.

4.   Describe how consumers' social relationships influence their decision making processes.

5.   Explain the prepurchase, purchase, and postpurchase activities consumers engage in when making decisions.

CHAPTER OUTLINE

Please refer to your textbook in order to define, list, and/or describe the missing parts of the chapter outline. The page numbers given will help guide you through this learning process.

I. DECISIONS, DECISIONS

Consumer Behavior _____ (p.147)

Involvement _____ (p.148)

Perceived Risk _____ (p.148)

   A. Problem Recognition _____ (p.149)

   B. Information Search _____ (p.149)

   C. Evaluation of Alternatives
      Evaluation Criteria _____ (p.150)

   D. Product Choice
      Heuristics _____ (p.151)

      Brand Loyalty _____ (p.151)

   E. Postpurchase Evaluation
      Customer Satisfaction/Dissatisfaction CS/D _____ (p.151)

II. INTERNAL INFLUENCES ON CONSUMER DECISIONS

   A. Perception _____ (p.152)

      Exposure _____ (p.152)

      Perceptual Selection _____ (p.153)

      Interpretations _____ (p.153)

   B. Motivation _____ (p.153)

      Hierarchy of Needs _____ (p.153)

   C. Learning _____ (p.155)

      1. Behavioral Learning
         Behavioral Learning Theories _____ (p.155)

         Classical Conditioning _____ (p.155)

         Operant Conditioning _____ (p.155)

Stimulus Generalization _____ (p.155)

    2.   Cognitive Learning
        Cognitive Learning Theory _____ (p.155)

D.   Attitudes _____ (p.155)

E.   Personality _____ (p.156)

    Innovativeness _____ (p.157)

    Self-Confidence _____ (p.157)

    Sociability _____ (p.157)

    Self-Concept _____ (p.157)

F.   Age Groups
        Family Life Cycle _____ (p.157)

G.   Lifestyles
        Lifestyle _____ (p.159)

    Psychographics _____ (p.159)

III. SITUATIONAL INFLUENCES ON CONSUMER DECISIONS
    A.   Physical Environment _____

    B.   Time _____

IV. SOCIAL INFLUENCES ON CONSUMER DECISIONS
    A.   Culture _____ (p.164)

    B.   Subcultures _____ (p.165)

    C.   Social Class _____ (p.165)

        Status Symbol _____ (p.165)

    D.   Group Behavior
        1.   Reference Group _____ (p.166)

            Conformity _____ (p.166)

            Sex Roles _____ (p.166)

        2.   Opinion Leaders
            Opinion Leader _____ (p.167)

74

CHAPTER 6

KEY TERMS

Select the correct term for each definition and write it in the space provided.

Learning
Social class
Consumer behavior
Opinion leader
Evaluative criteria
Personality
Culture
Brand Loyalty

Exposure
Subculture
Attitude
Motivation
Involvement
Perception
Family life-cycle

1. _Consumer behavior_ — The processes involved when individuals or groups select, purchase, use, and dispose of goods, services, ideas, or experiences to satisfy needs and desires. *(p.147)*

2. _Perception_ — The process by which people select, organize, and interpret stimuli to the five senses of sight, sound, smell, touch, and taste. *(p.152)*

3. _Exposure_ — The degree to which a marketing stimulus is within range of consumer's sensory receptors. *(p.152)*

4. _Brand Loyalty_ — A pattern of repeat product purchases, accompanied by an underlying positive attitude toward the brand, which is based on the belief that the brand makes products superior to its competition. *(p.151)*

5. _Motivation_ — An internal state that activates goal-directed behavior on the part of consumers in order to satisfy some need. *(p.153)*

6. _Learning_ — A relatively permanent change in the behavior of consumers that is caused by experience or acquired information. *(p.155)*

7. _Attitude_ — A learned predisposition to respond favorably or unfavorably to stimuli, based on relatively enduring evaluations of people, objects, and issues. *(p.155)*

8. _Personality_

The psychological characteristics that consistently influence the way a person responds to situations in his or her environment. *(p.156)*

9. _Life Cycle_

A means of characterizing consumers within a family structure based on different stages through which people pass as they grow older. *(p.157)*

10. _Culture_

The learned values and patterns of behavior that stem from the shared meanings, rituals, and traditions among the members of a society and that influence their attitudes, beliefs, preferences, and priorities toward abstract ideas, activities, and products. *(p.164)*

11. _Social Class_

The overall rank or social standing of groups of people within a society according to the value assigned to such factors as family background, education, occupation, and income. *(p.165)*

12. _Opinion Leader_

A person who is frequently able to influence others' attitudes or behaviors by virtue of their active interest and expertise in one or more product categories. *(p.167)*

13. _Subculture_

A group within a society whose members share a distinctive set of beliefs, characteristics, or common experiences. *(p.165)*

14. _Involvement_

The relative importance of the perceived consequences of the purchase to a consumer. *(p.148)*

15. _Evaluation Criteria_

The dimensions (or product characteristics) used to judge the merits of competing options. *(p.150)*

MULTIPLE CHOICE
Identify the most correct answer.

1. The stimulus must be within range of people's sensory receptors to be noticed is called: *(p.152)*
   a. perceptual selectivity.
   b. exposure.
   c. sensory overload.
   d. adaptation.

2. Learning that occurs as the result of rewards or punishments is called: *(p.155)*
   a. attitude conditioning.
   b. behavioral conditioning.
   c. classical conditioning.
   d. operant conditioning.

3. According to Abraham Maslow's Theory of Motivation, there exists: *(p.153)*
   a. a hierarchy of needs.
   b. essentially the person's conscience.
   c. the referee in the subconscious struggle between temptation and virtue.
   d. the opposing force to the superid.

4. According to Maslow's Hierarchy of Needs, the lowest level of importance is: *(p.154)*
   a. spiritual fulfillment.
   b. the basic needs for food, clothing, and shelter.
   c. social approval.
   d. a sense of family.

5. Theories of learning that stress the importance of internal mental processes and that view people as problem-solvers who actively use information from the world around them to master their environment are known as: *(p.155)*
   a. behavioral learning theories.
   b. classical conditioning.
   c. cognitive learning theories.
   d. positive reinforcement.

6. A behavioral theory suggesting that an attitude has three components--affect, behavior, and cognition--and emphasizing the interrelationships among knowing, feeling, and doing is the: *(p.156)*
   a. observational learning theory.
   b. trait theory.
   c. sociability theory.
   d. ABC model of attitudes.

7. Self concept is: *(p.157)*
   a. an individual's self-image that is composed of a mixture of beliefs, observations, and feelings about personal attributes.
   b. the degree to which a person has a positive evaluation of his/her abilities.
   c. the degree to which a person enjoys social interaction.
   d. none of the above.

8. The pattern of living that determines how people choose to spend their time, money, and energy and that reflects their values, tastes, and preferences is called: *(p.159)*
   a. life-cycle.
   b. personality.
   c. lifestyle.
   d. self-esteem.

9. A group within a society whose members share a distinctive set of beliefs, characteristics, or common experiences is a: *(p.165)*
   a. social class.
   b. subculture.
   c. reference group.
   d. norm.

10. The degree to which reference groups influence purchasing decisions is tied to: *(p.166)*
    a. marketing efforts that rely on superstars.
    b. decisions about specific brands.
    c. how socially conspicuous the purchase is to others.
    d. the latest trends and style.

11. The relative importance of perceived consequences of the purchase to a consumer is called: *(p.148)*
    a. involvement.
    b. perceived risk.
    c. attitude.
    d. all of the above.

12. Products that are purchased and displayed to signal membership in a desirable social class indicate: *(p.165)*
    a. a subculture.
    b. a social class.
    c. a culture.
    d. a status symbol.

13. The process where the consumer checks his or her memory and/or surveys his or her environment in order to collect the data required to make a reasonable decision is: *(p.149)*
    a. problem recognition.
    b. information search.
    c. perceived risk.
    d. habitual decision making.

14. A change in beliefs or actions as a reaction to real or imagined group pressure is called: *(p.166)*
    a. a team.
    b. an inference group.
    c. conformity.
    d. a social class.

15. Example(s) of heuristics include: *(p.151)*
    a. the belief that price equals quality.
    b. brand loyalty.
    c. mental shortcuts that lead to a speedy decision.
    d. all of the above.

CHAPTER IN REVIEW - WRITING TO LEARN

1. Discuss the role perception plays, as a factor that can influence consumer behavior.

_____

_____

_____

2. Identify the factors that influence purchasing decisions and buyer behavior.

_____

_____

_____

3. Discuss the role motivation plays, as a factor that can influence consumer behavior.

_____

_____

_____

A Case Analysis Exercise

Real People, Real Choices: Meet Richard Wertheimer, A decision Maker at the American Sheep Industry Association.

Reread the Opening Vignette on page 147 of your text and answer the following questions.

1.   Who is Richard Wertheimer?

2.   What is ASI?

3.   Identify the functions or activities carried out by the ASI.

4.   Describe the experience Richard Wertheimer offers as director of business development.

5.   Describe Richard Wertheimer's educational background.

ANSWERS
CHAPTER OUTLINE

I.   DECISIONS, DECISIONS
Consumer Behavior--The process involved when individuals or groups select, purchase, use and dispose of goods, services, ideas or experiences to satisfy their needs and desires.
Involvement--The relative importance of perceived consequences of the purchase to a consumer.
Perceived Risk--The belief that use of a product has potentially negative consequences, either financial, physical or social.
   A.   Problem Recognition--Occurs whenever the consumer sees a significant difference between his or her current state of affairs and some desired or ideal state; this recognition initiates the decision-making process.
   B.   Information Search--The process whereby a consumer searches for appropriate information to make a reasonable decision.
   C.   Evaluation of Alternatives
Evaluative Criteria--Dimensions used by consumers to compare competing product alternatives.
   D.   Product Choice
Heuristics--A mental rule of thumb that leads to a speedy decision by simplifying the process.
Brand Loyalty--A pattern of repeat product purchases, accompanied by an underlying positive attitude toward the brand, which is based on the belief that the brand makes products superior to its competition.

E.   Postpurchase Evaluation
     Consumer Satisfaction/Dissatisfaction CS/D--The overall feelings or attitudes a person has about a product after purchasing it.

II. INTERNAL INFLUENCES ON CONSUMER DECISIONS
     A.   Perception--The process by which people select, organize and interpret information from the outside world.
          Exposure--The stimulus must-be within range of people's sensory receptors to be noticed.
          Perceptual Selection--Consumers choose to pay some attention to some stimuli but not to others.
          Interpretation--Meaning is assigned to the stimulus.
     B.   Motivation--An internal state that drives us to satisfy needs by activating goal-oriented behavior.
          Hierarchy of Needs--An approach that categorizes motives according to five levels of importance, more basic needs being on the bottom of the hierarchy and the higher needs at the top.
     C.   Learning--A relatively permanent change in the behavior caused by acquired information or experience.
          1.   Behavioral Learning
               Behavioral Learning Theories--Theories of learning that focus on how consumer behavior is changed by external events or stimuli.
               Classical Conditioning--The learning that occurs when the stimulus eliciting a response is paired with another stimulus that initially does not elicit a response on its own but will cause a similar response over time because of its association with the first stimulus.
               Operant Conditioning--Learning that occurs as the result of rewards or punishments.
               Stimulus Generalization--Behavior caused by a reaction to one stimulus occurs in the presence of another, similar stimulus.
          2.   Cognitive Learning
               Cognitive Learning Theory--The theory of learning that stresses the importance of internal mental processes and that view people as problem-solvers who actively use information from the world around them to master their environment.
     D.   Attitude--A learned predisposition to respond favorably or unfavorably to stimuli based on relatively enduring evaluations of people, objects, and issues.
     E.   Personality--The psychological characteristics that consistently influence the way a person responds to situations in his or her environment.
          Innovativeness--The degree to which a person likes to try new things.

Self-Confidence--The degree to which a person has a positive evaluation of his or her own abilities.

Sociability--The degree to which a person enjoys social interaction.

Self-Concept--An individual's self-image that is composed of a mixture of beliefs, observations, and feelings about personal attributes.

    F.   Age Groups

Family Life Cycle--A means of characterizing consumers within a family structure based on different stages through which people pass as they grow older.

    G.   Lifestyles

Lifestyle--The pattern of living that determines how people choose to spend their time, money, and energy that reflects their values, tastes, and preferences.

Psychographics--The use of psychological, sociological, and anthropological factors to construct market segments.

III. SITUATIONAL INFLUENCES ON CONSUMER DECISIONS
    A.   Physical Environment
    B.   Time

IV. SOCIAL INFLUENCES ON CONSUMER DECISIONS
    A.   Culture--The values, beliefs and tastes valued by a group of people.
    B.   Subculture--A group within a society whose members share a distinctive set of beliefs, characteristics or common experience.
    C.   Social Class--The overall rank or social standing of groups of people within a society according to the value assigned to such factors as family, background, education, occupation and income.

Status Symbol--Products that are purchased and displayed to signal membership in desirable social class.

    D.   Group Behavior
        1.   Reference Group--An actual or imaginary individual or group that has a significant affect on an individuals evaluation s, aspirations or behavior.

Conformity--A change in beliefs or actions as a reaction to real or imagined group pressure.

Sex Roles--Society's expectations regarding the appropriate attitude, behaviors and appearance for men and women.

        2.   Opinion Leaders

Opinion Leader--A person who is frequently able to influence others' attitudes or behaviors by virtue of his or her active interests and expertise in one or more product categories.

KEY TERMS	MULTIPLE CHOICE

1.	Consumer behavior	1. b
2.	Perception	2. d
3.	Exposure	3. a
4.	Brand Loyalty	4. b
5.	Motivation	5. c
6.	Learning	6. d
7.	Attitude	7. a
8.	Personality	8. c
9.	Family life-cycle	9. b
10.	Culture	10. c
11.	Social class	11. a
12.	Opinion leader	12. d
13.	Subculture	13. b
14.	Involvement	14. c
15.	Evaluative criteria	15. d

CHAPTER IN REVIEW - WRITING TO LEARN

1. Perception is the process by which consumers select, organize and interpret the marketing stimuli to which they are exposed. To prevent sensory overload, consumers practice perceptual selectivity by choosing which stimuli they will pay attention to and which they will ignore.

2. Consumer purchasing decisions and buying behavior are influenced by many factors that include personal, social, and situational issues. The personal influences on consumers are important determinants of their needs and wants. Such factors as age, income, family status, and chosen lifestyle are strongly related to the types of products people buy and the specific brands they want.

3. Motivation is an internal state that drives us to satisfy needs. Once we activate a need, a state of tension exists that drives the consumer toward some goal that will reduce this tension by eliminating the need.

A CASE ANALYSIS EXERCISE

1. Richard Wertheimer is director of business development for the American Sheep Industry Association (ASI) based in Englewood, Colorado.

2. ASI is the promotion and marketing organization for the U.S. lamb and wool industry.

3. Specific activities carried out by the American Sheep Industry Association (ASI) include the forging of partnerships and the establishment of business-to-business marketing programs to stimulate the consumption of wool and lamb products in the United States and around the world.

4. Prior to assuming the position as director of business development in 1997, Wertheimer served the organization in various marketing capacities since 1983, including a stint as director of market services.

5. Richard Wertheimer received a B.S. degree in agricultural business management from the University of Wisconsin, Madison in 1982.

CHAPTER 7

WHY ORGANIZATIONS BUY: BUSINESS-TO-BUSINESS MARKETS

CHAPTER OVERVIEW

In this chapter, we learned about the general characteristics of business-to-business markets and business buying practices. Business-to-business markets include business and organizational customers who buy goods and services for purposes other than for personal consumption. Business and organizational customers are usually few in number, may be geographically concentrated, and often purchase higher priced products in larger quantities. Business buying practices include the decision of how a firm will utilize its suppliers, or sources, of the goods and services it needs. A firm's purchasing options include single sourcing, multiple sourcing, or systems buying.

Business and organizational markets are most frequently classified by the North American Industry Classification System (NAICS), a numerical coding system developed by NAFTA countries. More generally, business markets can be divided into the following major categories including producers, resellers, governments, and not-for-profit organizations.

Next, we reviewed how the business buy class identifies the degree and effort required to make a business buying decision. Purchase situations can be straight rebuy, modified rebuy, and new-task buying. A buying center is a group of people who work together to make a buying decision. The roles in the buying center are initiator, user, gatekeeper, influencer, decider, and buyer. The most important change in business buying is the growth of electronic commerce or e-commerce in which firms buy and sell products using the Internet, intranets, or extranets.

Lastly, the business buying decision process involves a number of stages that are similar but more complex than the steps followed by consumers when making a purchase decision. The recognition stage is accompanied by the submission of a purchase requisition and initiates the subsequent steps of developing product specifications, identifying potential suppliers, requesting and obtaining proposals, evaluating the proposals, selecting a supplier, placing the order, and finally, formal evaluation of the performance of the product and the supplier.

CHAPTER OBJECTIVES

1. Describe the general characteristics of business-to-business markets and business buying practices.

2. Tell how business and organizational markets are classified.

3. Explain the business buying situation and describe business buyers.

4. Understand the stages in the business buying decision process.

CHAPTER OUTLINE
Please refer to your textbook in order to define, list, and/or describe the missing parts of the chapter outline. The page numbers given will help guide you through this learning process.

I. BUSINESS MARKETS: BUYING AND SELLING WHEN STAKES ARE HIGH
Business-To-Business Marketing _____
_____ *(p.175)*

   A.   Characteristics That Make a Difference
      In Business Markets
      1.   Multiple Buyers _____ *(p.176)*
      2.   Number of Customers_____ *(p.177)*
      3.   Size of Purchases _____ *(p.177)*
      4.   Geographic Concentration_____ *(p.177)*
   B.   Business-to-Business Demand
      1.   Derived Demand_____ *(p.178)*
      2.   Inelastic Demand_____ *(p.179)*
      3.   Fluctuating Demand_____ *(p.180)*
          Acceleration Principle _____ *(p.180)*
      4.   Joint Demand_____ *(p.181)*

II. CLASSIFYING BUSINESS-TO-BUSINESS MARKETS_____
_____ *(p.181)*
North American Industry Classification System (NAICS)___
_____ *(p.181)*
   A.   Producers _____ *(p.182)*
   B.   Resellers _____ *(p.183)*
   C.   Governments
      Government Markets_____ *(p.183)*
      Competitive Bids _____ *(p.183)*
   D.   Not-For-Profit Institutions _____ *(p.184)*

III. THE NATURE OF BUSINESS BUYING _____
_____ *(p.184)*
   A.   The Buying Situation
      Buy Class_____ *(p.184)*
      1.   Straight Rebuy_____ *(p.184)*
      2.   Modified Rebuy_____ *(p.185)*
      3.   New-Task Buying_____ *(p.187)*
   B.   The Professional Buyer
      Centralized Purchasing _____ *(p.189)*
   C.   The Buying Center_____ *(p.189)*
      1.   The Fluid Nature of the Buying Center
      2.   Roles in the Buying Center
          Initiator_____ *(p.189)*
          User_____ *(p.189)*
          Gatekeeper_____ *(p.190)*

                Influencer_____ *(p.190)*
                Decider_____ *(p.190)*
                Buyer_____ *(p.190)*
    D.   Electronic Business-To-Business Commerce
          Electronic Commerce _____ *(p.190)*
          Intranet _____ *(p.191)*

IV. THE BUSINESS BUYING DECISION PROCESS
    A.   Problem Recognition_____ *(p.191)*
    B.   Information Search_____ *(p.192)*
          1.   Developing Product Specifications_____
                _____ *(p.192)*
          2.   Obtaining Proposals_____
                _____ *(p.192)*
    C.   Evaluation of Alternatives _____ *(p.193)*
    D.   Product and Supplier Selection _____
          _____ *(p.193)*
          Just-In-Time (JIT)_____ *(p.193)*
          Single Sourcing _____ *(p.193)*
          Multiple Sourcing _____ *(p.193)*
          Reciprocity _____ *(p.193)*
          Outsourcing_____ *(p.194)*
          Reverse Marketing _____ *(p.194)*
    E.   Postpurchase Evaluation_____
          _____ *(p.194)*

CHAPTER 7

KEY TERMS

Select the correct term for each definition and write it in the space provided.

Derived demand
Buying center
Not-for-profit institutions
Outsourcing
Competitive bids
Business-to-business marketing
Just-in-time (JIT)
Centralized purchasing

Buyer
Reseller market
Business and organizational
    customers
Modified rebuy
Single sourcing
Initiator
North American Industry
    Classification System (NAICS)

1. _____   Business firms and other organizations
                          that buy goods and services for some
                          purpose other than for personal
                          consumption. *(p.176)*

2. _____   Marketing activities that facilitate transactions involving goods and services that business and organizational customers need to produce other goods and services for resale and to support their operations. *(p.175)*

3. _____   Demand for business or organizational products derived from demand for consumer goods or services. *(p.178)*

4. _____   The business practice of buying a particular product from only one supplier. *(p.193)*

5. _____   The business buying practice of obtaining outside vendors to provide goods or services that otherwise might be supplied "in-house". *(p.194)*

6.   A business buying process in which two or more suppliers submit proposals (including price and associated data) for a proposed purchase and the firm providing the better offer is awarded the bid. *(p.183)*

7. _____   The numerical coding system that the United States, Canada, and Mexico use to classify firms into detailed categories according to their business activities and shared characteristics. *(p.181)*

8. _____   The individuals or organizations that buy finished goods for the purpose of reselling, renting, or leasing to others at a profit and for maintaining their business operations. *(p.183)*

9. _____   The organizations with charitable, educational, community, and other public-service goals that buy goods and services to support their functions and to attract and serve their members. *(p.184)*

10. _____   A business buying practice in which all organizational purchasing is performed by a central purchasing department. *(p.188)*

11. _____ A buying situation classification used by business buyers to categorize a previously made purchase that involves some change and that requires limited decision making. *(p.185)*

12. _____ The group of people in an organization who influence and participate in particular purchasing decisions. *(p.189)*

13. _____ The member of a business buying center who first recognizes that a purchase needs to be made and notifies others in the organization. *(p.189)*

14. _____ The member of a business buying center who has the formal authority and responsibility for executing the purchase. *(p.190)*

15. _____ Inventory management and purchasing practices used by manufacturers and resellers that reduce inventory and stock to very low levels, but assure deliveries from suppliers arrive just when needed. *(p.193)*

MULTIPLE CHOICE

Identify the most correct answer.

1. Characteristic(s) of the business market that complicates the marketing process in what makes these markets attractive in the first place including: *(p.175)*
   a. the size of the market.
   b. the volume of purchases.
   c. the concentration of potential customers in specific geographic regions.
   d. all of the above.

2. A small percentage change in consumer demand can create a large percentage change in total industrial or business demand which is known as: *(p.180)*
   a. the acceleration principle.
   b. inelastic demand.
   c. the ripple effect.
   d. indirect marketing.

3. Multiple sourcing is: *(p.193)*
   a. when two or more goods are used together to manufacture a product.
   b. the business practice of buying a particular product from several different suppliers.
   c. acquiring specialized services from outside suppliers.
   d. the business buying practice of obtaining outside vendors to provide goods or services that otherwise might be supplied "in-house".

4. A business buying practice in which organizations simplify the decision process by selecting a single supplier to provide everything needed for a complete production or operations system is called: *(p.193)*
   a. single sourcing.
   b. independent outsourcing.
   c. systems buying.
   d. sampling buying.

5. Inelastic demand: *(p.179)*
   a. means that a buyer and seller agree to be each other's customers.
   b. is a practice in which many of the functions of buyer and seller are reversed.
   c. means the demand for products that does not change because of increases or decreases in price.
   d. none of the above.

6. The Internal computer connections that organizations use to distribute information among a company's different offices and locations. *(p.191)*
   a. e-mail.
   b. Internet.
   c. e-commerce.
   d. Intranet.

7. The federal, state, county, and local governments that buy goods to carry out public objectives and to carry on their operations are known as: *(p.183)*
   a. public markets.
   b. government markets.
   c. institutional markets.
   d. community markets.

8. A buy class: *(p.184)*
   a. is identified by the degree of effort required to collect information and make a decision.
   b. is applied to three different buying situations.
   c. includes a straight rebuy, modified rebuy, and new-task buy.
   d. all of the above.

9. A buying situation classification used by business buyers to categorize routine purchases that require minimal decision making is a: *(p.184)*
   a. modified rebuy.
   b. new-task buy.
   c. straight rebuy.
   d. routine buy.

10. A new-task buy: *(p.187)*
   a. is the buying situation when a purchase is made for the very first time.
   b. is characterized by certainty and no risk.
   c. involves the least effort since the buyer has no previous experience on which to base a decision.
   d. all of the above.

11. A member of a business buying center who will actually use a business product after it is purchased is a(n): *(p.189)*
   a. initiator.
   b. decider.
   c. user.
   d. buyer.

12. The gatekeeper is the member of a business buying center who: *(p.190)*
   a. gives purchasing expertise.
   b. controls the flow of information to other members.
   c. first recognizes that a purchase needs to be made.
   d. controls the distribution of products purchased.

13. A member of a business buying center who affects the buying decision by dispensing advise or sharing expertise is called a(n): *(p.190)*
   a. influencer.
   b. buyer.
   c. initiator.
   d. mentor.

14. The decider: *(p.190)*
   a. is the member of the buying center who makes the final decision.
   b. may have formal or informal power to authorize spending the company's money.
   c. may be the purchasing agent or the CEO of an organization.
   d. all of the above.

15. The buying and selling of products electronically, usually via the Internet. *(p.190)*
    a. supplier quote.
    b. supplier search.
    c. Electronic commerce, or e-commerce.
    d. cost analysis.

CHAPTER IN REVIEW - WRITING TO LEARN

1. Describe the general characteristics of business-to-business markets.

   _____

   _____

   _____

2. Identify the three major categories of business markets.

   _____

   _____

   _____

3. Describe the function of a buying center in business buying behavior.

   _____

   _____

   _____

A Case Analysis Exercise

Real People, Real Choices: Meet Craig Weisbruch, A Decision Maker at National Gypsum Company.

Reread the Opening Vignette on page 174 of your text and answer the following questions.

1. What are some of Craig Weisbruch's duties as Senior Vice President of Sales & Marketing at the National Gypsum Company?

2. What was Craig Weisbruch's position in the company before he was promoted to Senior Vice President of Sales and Marketing, and what were his previous responsibilities?

3. What product does the National Gypsum Company produce, and how much of this product is contributed to the global market?

4. What year did Craig Weisbruch begin his career at National Gypsum and what position did he hold in the firm?

5. What was Craig Weisbruch's original major when he was graduated from Louisiana State University? What year did he graduate from this school?

ANSWERS
CHAPTER OUTLINE

I. BUSINESS MARKETS: BUYING AND SELLING WHEN STAKES ARE HIGH
    Business-to-Business Marketing--Marketing of those goods and services that business and organizational customers need to produce other goods and services for resale or to support their operations.
    A. Characteristics That Make a Difference In Business Markets
        1. Multiple Buyers--In business markets, products often have to do more than satisfy an individual's needs. They must meet the requirements of everyone involved in the company's purchase decision.
        2. Number of Customers--Business marketers have a narrow customer base and a small number of buyers.
        3. Size of Purchases--Business-to-Business products can dwarf consumer purchases, both in the quantity of items ordered and in the price of individual purchases.
        4. Geographic Concentration Meaning that many business customers are located in a small geographic area rather than being spread out across the country. Firms often choose to set up shop in areas that allow easy access to raw materials.

    B. Business-To-Business Demand
        1. Derived Demand--Demand for business or organizational products derived from demand for consumer goods or services.
        2. Inelastic Demand--Demand for products that does not change because of increases or decreases in price.
        3. Fluctuating Demand--When talking about demand coming from the end consumer, even small changes can create large increases or decreases in business demand.

Acceleration Principle--A marketing phenomenon in which a small percentage change in consumer demand can create a large percentage change in business-to-business demand.

4. Joint Demand--Demand for two or more goods that are used together to create a product.

II. CLASSIFYING BUSINESS-TO-BUSINESS MARKETS--Many firms buy products in business markets so they can produce other goods in turn.

North American Industry Classification System (NAICS)--The numerical coding system that the United States, Canada, and Mexico use to classify firms into detailed categories according to their business activities and shared characteristics.

A. Producers--The individuals or organizations that purchase products for use in the production of other goods and services.

B. Resellers--The individuals or organizations that buy finished goods for the purpose of reselling, renting, or leasing to others to make a profit and to maintain their business operations.

C. Governments

Government Markets--The federal, state, county and local governments that buy goods and services to carry out public objectives and to support their operations.

Competitive Bids--A business buying process in which two or more suppliers submit proposals (including price and associated data) for a proposed purchase and the firm providing the better offer gets the bid.

D. Not-For-Profit Institutions--The organizations with charitable, educational, community, and other public service goals that buy goods and services to support their functions and to attract and serve their members.

III. THE NATURE OF BUSINESS BUYING--To be successful in business-to-business markets means developing marketing strategies that meet the needs of organizational customers better than the competition.

A. The Buying Situation

Buy Class--One of three classifications of business buyers that characterizes the degree of time and effort required to make a decision in a buying situation.

1. Straight Rebuy--A buying situation in which business buyers make routine purchases that require minimal decision making.

2. Modified Rebuy--A buying situation classification used by business buyers to categorize a previously made purchase that involves some change and that requires limited decision making.

3. New-Task Buying--A new business-to-business purchase that is complex or risky and that requires extensive decision making.

B. The Professional Buyer
Centralized Purchasing--A business buying practice in which an organization purchasing department does the buying for all the company's facilities.
C. The Buying Center--The group of people in an organization who influences and participates in purchasing decisions.
1. The Fluid Nature of the Buying Center
2. Roles in the Buying Center
Initiator--Begins the buying process by first recognizing that the firm needs to make a purchase.
User--Is the member of the buying center who needs the purchased product
Gatekeeper--Is the member who controls the flow of information to other members
Influencer--Affects the buying decision by dispensing advice or sharing expertise
Decider--Is the member of the buying center who makes the final decision
Buyer--Is the person who has responsibility for executing the purchase
D. Electronic Business-To-Business Commerce
Electronic Commerce--The buying and selling of products electronically, usually via the Internet
Intranet--Internal computer connections that organizations use to distribute information among a company's different offices and locations.

IV. THE BUSINESS BUYING DECISION PROCESS
A. Problem Recognition--Occurs when someone sees that a purchase can solve a problem.
B. Information Search--Searching for information about products and suppliers.
1. Developing Product Specifications--A written description laying out their exact product requirements-the quality size, weight, color, etc.
2. Obtaining Proposals--The buyer's next step is to obtain written or verbal proposals, or bids, from one or more potential suppliers.
C. Evaluation of Alternatives--This stage is when the buying center assesses the proposals.
D. Product And Supplier Selection--The selection of the best product and supplier to meet the firm's needs.
Just-In-Time (JIT)--Inventory management and purchasing processes that manufacturers and resellers use to reduce inventory to very low levels and ensure that deliveries from suppliers arrive only when needed.
Single Sourcing--The business practice of buying a

particular product from only one supplier.

Multiple Sourcing--The business practice of buying a particular product from many suppliers.

Outsourcing--The business buying process of obtaining outside vendors to provide goods or services that otherwise might be supplied in-house.

Reverse Marketing--A business practice in which a buyer firm shapes a supplier's products and operations to satisfy its needs.

E. Postpurchase Evaluation--An organizational buyer assesses whether the performance of the product and the supplier is living up to expectations.

CHAPTER 7
ANSWERS

KEY TERMS   **MULTIPLE CHOICE**

1. Business and organizational customers   1. d
2. Business-to-business marketing   2. a
3. Derived demand   3. b
4. Single sourcing   4. a
5. Outsourcing   5. c
6. Competitive bids   6. d
7. North American Industry
    Classification System(NAICS)   7. b
8. Reseller market   8. d
9. Not-For-Profit Institutions   9. c
10. Centralized purchasing   10. a
11. Modified rebuy   11. c
12. Buying center   12. b
13. Initiator   13. a
14. Buyer   14. d
15. Just-in-time (JIT)   15. c

CHAPTER IN REVIEW - WRITING TO LEARN

1. Business-to-business markets include business and organizational customers who buy goods and services for purposes other than for personal consumption. Business and organizational customers are usually few in number, may be geographically concentrated, and often purchase higher priced products in larger quantities.

2. Business markets can be divided into the three major categories of producers, resellers, and organizations. Producers purchase materials, parts, and various goods and

services needed to produce other goods and services to be sold at a profit. Resellers purchase finished goods to resell at a profit, as well as other goods and services to maintain their operations. Governments and other non-profit organizations purchase the goods and services necessary to fulfill their objectives.

3. A buying center, or cross-functional team of decision makers, may be formed for a specific purchasing decision. Different members of the buying center usually take one or more roles: initiator, user, gatekeeper, influencer, decider, or buyer.

A CASE ANALYSIS EXERCISE

1. Craig Weisbruch's duties include product pricing, demand management, advertising, technical service, and product development.

2. Craig Weisbruch was Vice President of Marketing before he was promoted to Senior Vice President of Sales and Marketing. His previous responsibilities included new product development and product marketing.

3. National Gypsum is the world's second largest producer of gypsum wallboard.

4. Craig Weisbruch joined National Gypsum in 1994 as a sales representative.

5. Craig Weisbruch received his B.A. in history from Louisiana State University in 1971.

CHAPTER 8

SHARPENING THE FOCUS:
TARGET MARKETING STRATEGIES

CHAPTER OVERVIEW

The purpose of this chapter was to understand the need for market segmentation and target marketing in today's business environment. Market segmentation and target marketing are important strategies in today's marketplace due to the splintering of a mass society into diverse groups because of technological and cultural differences known as market fragmentation. Market segmentation means to divide a large market into a set of smaller markets that share important characteristics. In target marketing, marketers select one or more of these specific groups to serve.

In developing a segmentation strategy, marketers first examine consumer demand in relation to the product. If demand is homogenous, a mass market strategy where only one product is sold to the total market may be best. If demand is clustered or diffused, a segmented marketing strategy may be better. To choose one or more segments to target, marketers examine each segment and evaluate its potential for success as a target market.

Next, we considered the different dimensions used for segmenting consumer markets. Marketers frequently find it useful to segment consumer markets based on demographic characteristics including age, gender, family structure, social class, race or ethnic identity, geographic location, or geodemography. Consumer markets may also be segmented based on consumer lifestyles and how consumers behave toward the product.

Categories similar to those in the consumer market are frequently used for segmenting industrial markets. Industrial demographics include industry and/or company size, North American Industry Classification System (NAICS) codes or geographic location. Industrial markets may also be segmented based on operating variables, purchasing approaches, and end-use applications.

After the different segments have been identified, the market potential of each segment is estimated which influences the firm's selection of an overall marketing strategy. The firm may choose as undifferentiated, differentiated, concentrated, or custom strategy based on the company's characteristics and the nature of the market.

Finally, after the target market(s) and the overall strategy have been selected, marketers must determine how they wish the brand to be perceived by consumers relative to the competition such as should the brand be positioned like, against, or away from the competition. Marketers must continually monitor changes in the market which might indicate a need for repositioning of the product.

CHAPTER OBJECTIVES

1. Understand the three steps involved in developing a target marketing strategy.

2. Understand the need for market segmentation in today's business environment.

3. Know the different dimensions used for segmenting consumer markets.

4. Understand the bases for segmentation in industrial markets.

5. Explain how potential market segments are evaluated and selected.

6. Explain how a targeting strategy is developed.

7. Understand how a firm develops and implements a product positioning strategy.

CHAPTER OUTLINE

Please refer to your textbook in order to define, list, and/or describe the missing parts of the chapter outline. The page numbers given will help guide you through this learning process.

I. "HAVE IT YOUR WAY": SELECTING AND
    ENTERING A MARKET
    Market Fragmentation_____ (p.201)
    Target Marketing Strategy _____
    _____ (p.202)

II. SEGMENTATION _____
    _____ (p.202)
    Segmentation Variables _____
    _____ (p.202)
    A. Dimensions For Segmenting Consumer Markets
        1. Segmenting By Demographics
            Age_____ (p.204)
            Generation X _____ (p.204)
            Baby Boomers _____ (p.204)

            Gender _____ *(p.204)*
            Family Structure _____ *(p.204)*
            Income and Social Class _____ *(p.205)*
            Race and Ethnicity _____ *(p.205)*
            Geography _____ *(p.206)*
            Geodemography _____ *(p.206)*
      2.   Segmenting By Psychographics _____
            _____ *(p.207)*
            VALS 2 (Values and Lifestyles) _____
            _____ *(p.207)*
      3.   Segmenting By Behavior
            Behavioral Segmentation _____
            _____ *(p.207)*
            80/20 Rule _____ *(p.208)*
            Usage Occasions _____ *(p.208)*

    B.   Dimensions For Segmenting Industrial Markets
        1.   Organizational Demographics _____ *(p.209)*
        2.   Company-Specific Characteristics_____
            _____ *(p.210)*
            Operating Variables _____
            _____ *(p.210)*

III. TARGETING
    Target Market _____ *(p.210)*
    A.   Evaluate Market Segments
        1. _____ *(p.211)*
        2. _____ *(p.211)*
        3. _____ *(p.211)*
        4. _____ *(p.211)*
        5. _____ *(p.211)*
    B.   Develop Segment Profiles
        Segment Profile _____ *(p.211)*
        Market Potential _____ *(p.212)*
    C.   Choose A Targeting Strategy
        1.   Undifferentiated Marketing
            Undifferentiated Targeting Strategy _____
            _____ *(p.212)*
        2.   Differentiated Marketing
            Differentiated Targeting Strategy _____
            _____ *(p.212)*
        3.   Concentrated Marketing
            Concentrated Targeting Strategy _____
            _____ *(p.213)*
        4.   Custom Marketing: A "Segment of One"
            Custom Marketing Strategy _____
            _____ *(p.215)*
            Mass Customization _____
            _____ *(p.216)*

IV. POSITIONING _____ (p.216)
    A.   Develop A Positioning Strategy _____
                                                        (p.216)
        1.   Analyze Competitors' Positions_____
                                                        (p.216)
        2.   Identify Competitive Advantage _____
                                                        (p.216)
        3.   Finalize The Marketing Mix _____
                                                        (p.217)
        4.   Evaluate The Target Market's Responses
              And Modify The Strategy _____ (p.217)
              Repositioning _____ (p.217)
    B.   Positioning Dimensions _____ (p.217)
        1.   Bringing A Product To Life: The Brand_____
              Personality_____ (p.217)
        2.   Perceptual Mapping _____ (p.218)

CHAPTER 8

KEY TERMS

Select the correct term for each definition and write it in the space provided.

Operating variables   Segmentation
Market potential   Brand personality
Target marketing strategy   Concentrated targeting
                                         strategy
Perceptual map   Segmentation variables
Geodemography   Custom marketing strategy
Positioning   Usage occasions
Differentiated targeting   VALS 2 (Values and Lifestyles)
    strategy
Market fragmentation

1. _____   A condition in society in which people
                        are divided into many different groups
                        with distinct needs and wants. *(p.201)*

2. _____   A market strategy in which a firm seeks
                        to serve the needs of one or more
                        different segments. *(p.202)*

3. _____   A process whereby marketers divide a
                        large customer group into segments that
                        share important characteristics. *(p.202)*

4. _____   An indicator that is used in one type of
                        market segmentation based on when
                        consumers use a product most. *(p.208)*

5. _____ The production technology used, the business customer's degree of technical, financial, or operations expertise, and whether or not the prospect is a current user or nonuser of the product. *(p.210)*

6. _____ Characteristics of customers that will allow the total market to be divided into fairly homogenous groups, each with different needs that can be profitably met by a firm. *(p.202)*

7. _____ A way to segment consumer markets based on geography combined with demographics. *(p.206)*

8. _____ A psychographic system that divides the entire U.S. population into eight segments. *(p.207)*

9. _____ The maximum demand expected among consumers in a potential market segment for a good or service. *(p.212)*

10. _____ A marketing strategy in which a firm develops one or more products for each of several distinct customer groups. *(p.212)*

11. _____ A marketing strategy in which a firm focuses its efforts on offering one or more products to a single segment. *(p.213)*

12. _____ A marketing strategy in which a firm develops a separate marketing mix for each customer. *(p.215)*

13. _____ The marketing practice of determining how a brand is perceived by consumers relative to the competition. *(p.216)*

14. _____ A distinctive image created for a brand that captures its character and the benefits it delivers. *(p.217)*

15. _____ A research technique which constructs a graphical representation of where products or brands are "located" in relation to each other in consumers' minds. *(p.218)*

MULTIPLE CHOICE
Identify the most correct answer.

1. _____ _____ occurs when people's diverse interests and backgrounds have divided them into different groups with distinct needs and wants. *(p.201)*
   a. broadcasting.
   b. mass marketing.
   c. segmenting.
   d. market fragmentation.

2. A positioning strategy: *(p.216)*
   a. divides the overall market into market segments.
   b. involves the creation of a marketing mix that is calculated to most closely match the needs of the target market segment.
   c. provides a comparative advantage over rival offerings in the minds of the segment members.
   d. all of the above.

3. The segment of people who are in their thirties and forties is called: *(p.204)*
   a. baby boomers.
   b. Generation X.
   c. baby busters.
   d. Generation Z.

4. For a demand segment to be usable, it should satisfy the following criterion/criteria: *(p.211)*
   a. Can the segment be measured and understood?
   b. Is the segment large enough to be profitable, now and in the future?
   c. Can the marketer adequately serve the needs of the segment?
   d. All of the above.

5. The measurable characteristics of a population are: *(p.203)*
   a. geographics.
   b. geneologies.
   c. demographics.
   d. generations.

6. The following factors make the Hispanic segment attractive to marketers: *(p.206)*
   a. Hispanics are not brand-loyal.
   b. They tend to be highly concentrated by national origin, which makes it easy to identify subsegments.
   c. The average Hispanic household contains 2.7 people, compared to 3.5 people for the rest of the U.S.
   d. All of the above.

7. A way to segment consumer markets based on how they act toward, feel about, or use a good or service is called: *(p.207)*
   a. behavioral segmentation.
   b. geodemography.
   c. lifestyle segmentation.
   d. VALS 2.

8. Behavioral segmentation means: *(p.207)*
   a. consumers make a conscious decision to keep buying the same brand.
   b. dividing consumers into segments on the basis of how they act toward, feel about, or use a product or service.
   c. consumers make a purchase out of habit.
   d. consumers will vary in terms of their current interest in purchasing a product.

9. A description of the "typical" customer in a market segment. *(p.211)*
   a. segment fragment.
   b. fragment target.
   c. custom profile.
   d. segment profile.

10. A marketing strategy that assumes that the majority of customers have similar needs and attempts to appeal to a broad spectrum of people is known as a(n): *(p.212)*
    a. differentiated marketing strategy.
    b. counter segmentation.
    c. undifferentiated marketing strategy.
    d. maximized marketing strategy.

11. A target market is a: *(p.210)*
    a. group or groups selected by a firm to be turned into customers as a result of segmentation and targeting.
    b. market in which a firm focuses its efforts on offering one or more products to several segments.
    c. market in which a firm develops a separate marketing mix for each customer.
    d. all of the above.

12. A marketing strategy in which a firm modifies a basic good or service to meet the needs of an individual customer is called: *(p.216)*
    a. differentiated marketing strategy.
    b. mass customization.
    c. unique segmentation.
    d. modified marketing strategy.

13. The following guideline(s) often apply to effective targeting strategies: *(p.212)*
    a. An undifferentiated strategy is often appropriate for products that people perceive as basically homogenous.
    b. A concentrated or custom strategy is often useful for smaller firms that do not have the resources or the desire to be all things to all people.
    c. The choice of a strategy tends to change as the product moves through the life cycle.
    d. All of the above.

14. A marketing rule of thumb that 20 percent of purchasers account for 80 percent of a product's sales is called the: *(p.208)*
    a. 20/80 rule.
    b. market percentage rule.
    c. 80/20 rule.
    d. target market rule.

15. When a brand's original "personality" is altered, often to appeal to a different market segment, it is called: *(p.217)*
    a. repositioning.
    b. image advantage strategy.
    c. adjustment segmentation.
    d. competitive identification.

CHAPTER IN REVIEW - WRITING TO LEARN
1. Describe market segmentation and target marketing.

_____

_____

_____

2. Identify the bases for segmentation in industrial markets.

_____

_____

_____

3. Explain how potential market segments are evaluated and selected.

_____

_____

_____

A Case Analysis Exercise

Real People, Real Choices: Meet Sarah Burroughs, A Decision Maker at Burrell Communications

Reread the Opening Vignette on page 201 of your text and answer the following questions.

1. Who is Sarah Burroughs, and what are her responsibilities at the Burrell Communications Group?

2. Describe Ms. Burroughs' career.

3. When was Ms. Burroughs promoted to Vice President?

4. Where did Ms. Burroughs attend college?

5. How has Burrell Communications Group served the McDonald's Corporation?

ANSWERS
CHAPTER OUTLINE

I.   "HAVE IT YOUR WAY": SELECTING AND ENTERING A MARKET
     Market Fragmentation--Condition of many consumer groups due to a diversity of distinct needs and wants in modern society.
     Target Marketing Strategy--Dividing the total market into different segments based on customer characteristics, selecting one or more segments, and developing products to meet the needs of those specific segments.

II. SEGMENTATION--The process of dividing a larger market into smaller pieces based on one or more meaningful, shared characteristics.
     Segmentation Variables--Divide the total market into fairly homogeneous groups, each with different needs and preferences.
     A.   Dimensions For Segmenting Consumer Markets
          1.   Segmenting By Demographics
               Age--Consumers of different age groups have very different needs and wants.
               Generation X--The group of consumers between the ages of 18 and 29.
               Baby Boomers--Segment of people who are in their thirties and forties.
               Gender--Many products appear to either men or women, thus segmenting the market by sex.
               Family Structure--Family needs and expenditures change over time, as well as the stage of the family life cycle.

Income and Social Class--The distribution of wealth is of great interest to marketers because it determines which groups have the greatest buying power.

Race and Ethnicity--A consumer's national origin is often a very strong indicator of his or her preferences in the market.

Geography--People's preferences often vary depending on where they live.

Geodemography--Technique used by marketers to segment markets that combines geography with demographics.

   2. Segmenting By Psychographics--Segmenting the market in terms of shared attitudes, interests, and opinions.

VALS 2 (Values and Lifestyles)--Psychographic system that divides the entire U.S. population into eight segments.

   3. Segmenting By Behavior

Behavioral Segmentation--Technique that divides consumers into segments on the basis of how they act toward, feel about, or use a product or service.

80/20 Rule--A marketing rule of thumb that 20 percent of purchasers account for 80 percent of a product's sales.

Usage Occasions--Indicator used in one type of market segmentation based on when consumers use a product most.

B. Dimensions For Segmenting Industrial Markets
   1. Organizational Demographics--Many industries use the North American Industry Classification System (NAICS) to learn more about a particular industry.
   2. Company-Specific Characteristics--Each firm has certain characteristics that influence the types of products and services it needs.

Operating Variables--The production technology used, the business customer's degree of technical, financial, or operations expertise, and whether or not the prospect is a current user or nonuser of the product.

III. TARGETING
   Target Markets--Group or groups selected by a firm to be turned into customers as a result of segmentation and targeting.
   A. Evaluate Market Segments
      1. Are members of the segment similar to each other in their product needs and wants and at the same time, different from consumers in other segments?
      2. Can marketers measure the segment?

3. Is the segment large enough to be profitable now and in the future?
4. Can marketing communications reach the segment?
5. Can the marketer adequately serve the needs of the segment?

B. Develop Segment Profiles
   Segment Profile--A description of the "typical" customer in a segment.
   Market Potential--The maximum demand expected among consumers in a segment for a product or service.

C. Choose A Targeting Strategy
   1. Undifferentiated Marketing
      Undifferentiated Targeting Strategy--Technique of attempting to appeal to a broad spectrum of people.
   2. Differentiated Marketing
      Differentiated Targeting Strategy--Developing one or more products for each of several distinct customer group sand making sure these offerings are kept separate in the marketplace.
   3. Concentrated Marketing
      Concentrated Targeting Strategy--Focusing a firm's efforts on offering one or more products to a single segment.
   4. Custom Marketing: A "Segment Of One"
      Custom Marketing Strategy--Approach that tailors specific products and the messages about them to individual customers.
      Mass Customization--Approach that modifies a basic product or service to meet the needs of an individual.

IV. POSITIONING--Developing a marketing strategy aimed at influencing how a particular market segment perceives a product or service in comparison to the competition.
   A. Developing A Positioning Strategy--The success of a target marketing strategy hinges on marketers' abilities to identify and select an appropriate market segment.
      1. Analyze Competitors' Positions--What competitors are out there, and how are they perceived by the target market?
      2. Identify Competitive Advantage--To provide a reason why consumers will perceive the product as better than the competition.
      3. Finalize The Marketing Mix--The elements of the marketing mix must match the selected segment.
      4. Evaluate The Target Market's Responses And Modify The Strategy--The firm may find that it needs to change which segments it targets, and the needs of people may change as well.
         Repositioning--Redoing a product's position to respond to marketplace changes.

B. Positioning Dimensions--Lifestyle image, Price leadership, Attributes, Product class, Competitors, Occasions, Users, and Quality.
   1. Bringing A Product To Life: The Brand Personality-- A distinctive image that captures a product or service's character and benefits.
   2. Perceptual Mapping--A vivid way to construct a picture of where products or brands are "located" in consumers' minds.

CHAPTER 8
ANSWERS

KEY TERMS

1. Market fragmentation
2. Target marketing strategy
3. Segmentation
4. Usage occasions
5. Operating variables
6. Segmentation variables
7. Geodemography
8. VALS 2 (Values and Lifestyles)
9. Market potential
10. Differentiated targeting strategy
11. Concentrated targeting strategy
12. Custom marketing strategy
13. Positioning
14. Brand personality
15. Perceptual map

MULTIPLE CHOICE

1. d
2. b
3. a
4. d
5. c
6. b
7. a
8. b
9. d
10. c
11. a
12. b
13. d
14. c
15. a

CHAPTER IN REVIEW - WRITING TO LEARN

1. Market segmentation means to divide a large market into a set of smaller markets that share important characteristics. In target marketing, marketers select one or more of these specific groups to serve. The development of a clear and positive image to communicate to members of the target market groups is called positioning.

2. Categories similar to those in the consumer market are frequently used for segmenting industrial markets. Industrial demographics including industry and/or company size, Standard Industrial Classification (SIC) codes or geographic location. Industrial markets may also be segmented based on operating variables, purchasing approaches, and end use applications.

3. After the different segments have been identified, the market potential of each segment is estimated. The relative attractiveness of segments is also influenced by the firm's selection of an overall marketing strategy. The firm may choose an undifferentiated, differentiated, concentrated, niche, or custom strategy based on the company's characteristics and the nature of the market.

A CASE ANALYSIS EXERCISE

1. As President and Chief Operating Officer of Burrell Communications Group, Sarah Burroughs is a key decision-maker for the country's largest minority-owned advertising agency.

2. Ms. Burroughs began her advertising career in 1964 at Foote, Cone, and Belding/Chicago, where she started out as an analytic assistant/typist and worked her way up through the company's ranks.

3. In 1971, she was promoted to Vice President/Associate Research Director, making her the youngest person to be named a vice president in the agency's history.

4. She is an alumnus of Lincoln University in Jefferson City, Missouri, where she earned a Bachelor of Arts degree in history.

5. The company has created advertising for McDonald's targeted to black consumers since 1972.

CHAPTER 9

THE PRODUCT

CHAPTER OVERVIEW

We began this chapter by defining the three dimensions of a product. The core product is the basic product category benefits and customized benefit(s) the product provides. The actual product is the physical good or delivered service including the packaging and brand name. The augmented product includes both the actual product and any supplementary services such as warranty, credit, delivery, installation, etc.

Next, we described the ways in which products are classified. Consumer products are classified according to how long they last including durable goods which provide benefits for months or years and nondurable goods which are used up quickly or are useful for only a short time. Consumer products are also classified by how they are purchased including convenience products, shopping products, specialty products, and unsought products. Business products are for commercial uses by organizations and are classified according to how they are used. New products are anything consumers perceive to be new and may be classified as to their degree of newness including continuous innovation, dynamically continuous innovation, and discontinuous innovation.

We then discussed the process of product adoption and the diffusion process. Product adoption is the process by which an individual begins to use a new product while the diffusion of innovations is how a new product spreads through a population. The stages in the adoption process are awareness, interest, evaluation, trial, adoption, and confirmation. Individuals may be classified according to their readiness to adopt new products including innovators, early adopters, early majority, late majority, and laggards. Five product characteristics that have an important effect on how quickly (or if) a new product will be adopted by consumers are relative advantage, compatibility, product complexity, trialability, and product observability.

CHAPTER OBJECTIVES

1. Explain the layers of a product.

2. Describe the classification of products.

3. Explain the importance of new products.

4. Describe how firms develop new products.

5. Explain the process of product adoption and the diffusion of innovations.

CHAPTER OUTLINE

Please refer to your textbook in order to define, list, and/or describe the missing parts of the chapter outline. The page numbers given will help guide you through this learning process.

I. BUILD A BETTER MOUSETRAP
   Goods _____ (p.231)
   A. Layers Of The Product Concept
      1. The Core Product _____ (p.232)
      2. The Actual Product _____ (p.233)
      3. The Augmented Product _____ (p.233)

II. CLASSIFYING PRODUCTS
   A. Consumer Product Classes Defined By How Long
      A Product Lasts
      Durable Goods _____ (p.233)
      Nondurable Goods _____ (p.233)
   B. Consumer Product Classes Defined By How Consumers
      Buy The Product
      Convenience Product _____ (p.235)
      Shopping Product _____ (p.235)
      Specialty Product _____ (p.236)
   C. Business-to-Business Products
      Equipment _____ (p.237)
      Maintenance, Repair, and Operating (MRO) Products ___
      _____ (p.237)
      Raw Materials _____ (p.237)
      Processed Materials _____ (p.237)
      Specialized Services _____ (p.237)
      Component Parts _____ (p.237)

III. IT'S NEW AND IMPROVED! UNDERSTANDING INNOVATIONS
   Innovations _____ (p.238)
   A. The Importance of Understanding Innovations _____
      _____ (p.238)
   B. Types of Innovations _____ (p.238)
      1. Continuous Innovation _____ (p.239)
         Knockoff _____ (p.239)
      2. Dynamically Continuous Innovation _____ (p.240)

      3. Discontinuous Innovation _____ (p.240)

IV. DEVELOPING NEW PRODUCTS _____ (p.242)
   A. The Visionary Phase _____ (p.242)
   B. Planning and Development _____ (p.243)
      Commercial Development _____ (p.243)
      Technical Development _____ (p.244)
   C. Testing and Improving the Product
      Test Marketing _____ (p.244)

V.   ADOPTION AND DIFFUSION PROCESSES
      Product Adoption_____ (p.246)
      Diffusion _____ (p.246)
      A.   Stages in a Customer's Adoption of a New Product____
            _____ (p.246)
            1.   Awareness_____ (p.247)
            2.   Interest_____ (p.247)
            3.   Evaluation_____ (p.247)
            4.   Trial_____ (p.248)
            5.   Adoption_____ (p.249)
            6.   Confirmation_____ (p.249)
      B.   The Diffusion Of Innovations _____ (p.249)
            1.   Adopter Categories
                  Innovators _____ (p.249)
                  Early Adopters _____ (p.250)
                  Early Majority _____ (p.250)
                  Late Majority _____ (p.250)
                  Laggards _____ (p.251)
            2.   Product Factors Affecting the Rate of Adoption
                  Relative Advantage_____ (p.251)
                  Compatibility_____ (p.252)
                  Complexity_____ (p.252)
                  Trialability_____ (p.252)
                  Observability_____ (p.252)
      C.   Organizational Differences Affect Adoption_____
            _____ (p.253)

CHAPTER 9

KEY TERMS
Select the correct term for each definition and write it in the space provided.

Specialty product
Discontinuous innovation
Goods
Innovators
Durable goods
Continuous innovation
Processed materials
Equipment

Laggards
Innovation
Raw materials
Convenience product
Diffusion
Component parts
Early majority

1. _____   Tangible products, that is, ones that can be seen, touched, smelled and/or tasted. *(p.231)*

2. _____   Manufactured goods or subassemblies of finished items that organizations need to complete their own products. *(p.237)*

3. _____ Consumer products that provide benefits over a period of time such as cars, furniture, and appliances. *(p.233)*

4. _____ A consumer good or service which is usually low-priced, widely available, and purchased frequently, with a minimum of comparison and effort. *(p.235)*

5. _____ A good or service which has unique characteristics, is very important to the buyer, and for which the buyer will devote significant effort to acquire. *(p.236)*

6. _____ A product (a good, service, or idea) that is perceived to be new and different from existing products. *(p.238)*

7. _____ A modification of an existing product used to set one brand apart from its competitors. *(p.239)*

8. _____ A totally new product that creates major changes in the way we live. *(p.240)*

9. _____ The process by which the use of an innovation spreads throughout a society or a population. *(p.246)*

10. _____ The first segment (roughly 2.5%) of a population to adopt a product. *(p.249)*

11. _____ The approximately 34% of the population whose adoption of a new product signals a general acceptance of the innovation. *(p.250)*

12. _____ The roughly 16% of consumers who are the last to adopt an innovation. *(p.251)*

13. _____ Expensive goods an organization uses in its daily operations that last for a long time. *(p.237)*

14. _____ Products created when firms transform raw materials from their original state. *(p.237)*

15. _____ Products of the fishing, lumber, agricultural, and mining industries that organizational customers purchase to use in their finished products. *(p.237)*

MULTIPLE CHOICE
Identify the most correct answer.

1. The outcome sought by a customer that motivates buying behavior; the value the customer receives from owning, using, or experiencing a product is known as: *(p.232)*
   a. the product promotion.
   b. product augmentation.
   c. the benefit of a product.
   d. the product desirability.

2. Consumer products that provide benefits for only a short time because they are consumed (such as food) or are no longer useful (such as newspapers) are: *(p.233)*
   a. convenience products.
   b. durable goods.
   c. disposable products.
   d. nondurable goods.

3. A shopping product is: *(p.235)*
   a. a good or service for which consumers will spend considerable time and effort gathering information and comparing a number of different alternatives before making a purchase.
   b. a consumer good or service which is usually low-priced, widely available, and purchased frequently, with a minimum of comparison and effort.
   c. a good or service which has unique characteristics, is very important to the buyer, and for which the buyer will devote significant effort to acquire.
   d. a product that is only needed and purchased when necessary.

4. A good or service for a consumer has little awareness or interest until the product or a need for the product is brought to his/her attention is called a(n): *(p.236)*
   a. convenience product.
   b. unsought product.
   c. innovation.
   d. specialty product.

5. A knockoff is: *(p.239)*
    a. a new product that has not been accepted by consumers.
    b. a reduction in the initial pricing of a product.
    c. a style that has deliberately been copied and modified, often with the intent to sell to a larger or different market.
    d. a new type of bug spray.

6. A continuous innovation: *(p.239)*
    a. is a more pronounced change in an existing product.
    b. will have a modest impact on the way people do things, creating some behavioral changes.
    c. includes such products as a self-focusing 35mm cameras and a 900 MHz cordless telephone.
    d. all of the above.

7. The process by which a consumer or business customer begins to use a good, service, or an idea is known as: *(p.246)*
    a. product adoption.
    b. product diffusion.
    c. product adaptation.
    d. product availability.

8. The first necessary step in the product adoption process is: *(p.248)*
    a. interest.
    b. awareness of the innovation.
    c. evaluation.
    d. trial.

9. The approximately 13.5% of adopters who adopt an innovation very early in the diffusion process but after the innovators are: *(p.250)*
    a. early majority.
    b. late innovators.
    c. first-time buyers.
    d. early adopters.

10. The roughly 34% of adopters who are willing to try new products only when there is little or no risk associated with the purchase, when the purchase becomes an economic necessity or when there is social pressure to purchase are: *(p.250)*
    a. laggards.
    b. early majority.
    c. late majority.
    d. pressure adopters.

11. The degree to which a new product is perceived to provide benefits superior to those provided by the product it replaces is called: *(p.251)*
    a.   comparative advantage.
    b.   relative advantage.
    c.   competitive advantage.
    d.   absolute advantage.

12. The extent to which a new product is consistent with existing cultural values, customers, and practices is: *(p.252)*
    a.   compatibility.
    b.   adaptability.
    c.   complexity.
    d.   convenience.

13. Observability refers to: *(p.252)*
    a.   the degree to which individuals find a new product or its use difficult to understand.
    b.   the ease of sampling a new product and its benefits.
    c.   how visible a new product and its benefits are to others who might adopt the innovation.
    d.   how the firm has marketed its product to the target market.

14. The degree to which consumers find a new product or its use difficult to understand refers to a product's: *(p.252)*
    a.   trialability.
    b.   complexity.
    c.   compatibility.
    d.   observability.

15. The ease of sampling a new product and its benefits is: *(p.252)*
    a.   observability.
    b.   complexity.
    c.   compatibility.
    d.   trialability.

CHAPTER IN REVIEW - WRITING TO LEARN
1.   Explain the three dimensions of a product.

_____

_____

_____

2.   Describe the product classifications of consumer products.

_____

_____

_____

3.   What are the five product characteristics that have an important effect on how quickly (or if) a new product will be adopted by consumers?

_____

_____

_____

A Case Analysis Exercise

Real People, Real Choices: Meet William K. Smith, A Decision Maker at Eastman Kodak Company

Reread the Opening Vignette on page 230 of your text and answer the following questions.

1.   What kind of experience has Mr. Smith utilized to his advantage?

2.   Describe Mr. Smith's educational background.

3.   What position does Mr. Smith hold at the Eastman Kodak Company?

4.   What other positions has Mr. Smith held?

5.   Has Mr. Smith been employed anywhere else besides the Eastman Kodak Company?

ANSWERS
CHAPTER OUTLINE

I.   BUILD A BETTER MOUSETRAP
     Goods--Tangible products we can see, touch, smell, hear, or taste.
     A.   Layers Of The Product Concept
          1.   The Core Product--Consists of all the benefits the product will provide for consumers or business customers.
          2.   The Actual Product--Is the physical good or the

delivered service that supplied the desired benefit.

3. The Augmented Product--The actual product plus other supporting features such as a warranty, credit, delivery, installation, and repair service after the sale.

II. CLASSIFYING PRODUCTS

A. Consumer Product Classes Defined By How Long A Product Lasts.

Durable Goods--Consumer products that provide benefits over a period of time such as cars, furniture, and appliances.

Non-durable Goods--Consumer products that provide benefits for a short time because they are consumed (such as food) or are no longer useful (such as newspapers).

B. Consumer Product Classes Defined By How Consumers Buy the Product

Convenience Product--A consumer good or service that is usually low priced, widely available, and purchased frequently, with a minimum of comparison and effort.

Shopping Product--A good or service for which consumers will spend considerable time and effort gathering information and comparing alternatives before making a purchase.

Specialty Product--A good or service that has unique characteristics, is important to the buyer, and for which the buyer will devote significant effort to acquire.

C. Business-to-Business Products

Equipment--Expensive goods an organization uses in its daily operations that last for a long time.

Maintenance, Repair, and Operating (MRO) Products--Goods That a business customer consumes in a relatively short time.

Raw Materials--Products of the fishing, lumber, agricultural, and mining industries that organizational customers purchase to use in their finished product.

Processed Materials--Products created when firms transform raw materials from their original state.

Specialized Services--Services purchased from outside suppliers that are essential to the operation of an organization but are not part of the production of a product.

Component Parts--Manufactured goods or subassemblies of finished items that organizations need to complete their own products.

III. IT'S NEW AND IMPROVED! UNDERSTANDING INNOVATIONS
Innovation--A product that consumers perceive to be new and different from existing products.
   A.   The Importance of Understanding Innovations--Technology is advancing at a dizzying pace. In addition, the high cost of developing new products and the even higher cost of new products that fail can be a serious concern.
   B.   Types of Innovations.
        Innovations--Differ in their degree of newness, and this helps to determine how quickly the products will be adopted by many members of a target market.
        1.   Continuous Innovation--A modification of an existing product that sets one brand apart from its competitors.
             Knockoff--A new product that copies with slight modification the design of an original product.
        2.   Dynamically Continuous Innovation--A change in an existing product that requires a moderate amount of learning or behavior change.
        3.   Discontinuous Innovation--A totally new product that creates major changes in the way we live.

IV. DEVELOPING NEW PRODUCTS--New-product development occurs in three phases.
   A.   The Visionary Phase--In the visionary phase of product development, marketers generate new-product ideas, screen new-product concepts, and complete a business analysis.
   B.   Planning And Development--If it survives the scrutiny of a business analysis, a new-product concept then undergoes commercial and technical development.
        Commercial Development--Means putting together a marketing plan that builds on the initial projections made during product screening and business analysis.
        Technical Development--Those involved in the process must, for example, determine which parts of a finished good the company will make and which ones will be bought from other suppliers.
   C.   Testing And Improving The Product
        Test Marketing--Testing the complete plan in a small geographic area that is similar to the larger market the firm hopes to enter.

V.   ADOPTION AND DIFFUSION PROCESSES
     Product Adoption--The process by which a consumer or business customers begins to buy and use a new good, service, or an idea.
     Diffusion--The process by which the use of a product spreads throughout a population.

A. Stages in a Customer's Adoption of a New Product--Individuals and organizations pass through six stages in the adoption process.
   1. Awareness--Learning that the innovation exists is the first step in the adoption process.
   2. Interest--A prospective adopter begins to see how a new product might satisfy an existing or newly realized need.
   3. Evaluation--In the evaluation stage, a prospect weighs the costs and benefits of a new product.
   4. Trial--The potential adopters will actually experience or use the product for the first time.
   5. Adoption--A prospect chooses a product.
   6. Confirmation--Favorable experiences contribute to a new customers becoming loyal adopters.
B. The Diffusion Of Innovations--Describes how the use of a product spreads throughout a population.
   1. Adopter Categories
      Innovators--The first segment (roughly 2.5 percent) of a population to adopt a new product.
      Early Adopters--Those who adopt an innovation early in the diffusion process but after the innovators.
      Early Majority--Those whose adoption of a new product signals a general acceptance of the innovation.
      Late Majority--The adopters who are willing to try new products only when there is little or no risk associated with the purchase, when the purchase becomes an economic necessity or when there is social pressure to purchase.
      Laggards--The last consumers to adopt an innovation.
   2. Product Factors Affecting the Rate of Adoption
      Relative Advantage—The degree to which a consumer perceives that a new product provides superior benefits.
      Compatibility--The extent to which a new product is consistent with existing cultural values, customs, and practices.
      Complexity--The degree to which consumers find a new product or its use difficult to understand.
      Trialability--The ease of sampling a new product and its benefits.
      Observability--How visible a new product and its benefits are to others who might adopt it.
C. Organizational Differences Affect Adoption--Businesses and other organizations are not alike in their willingness to buy and use new industrial products.

KEY TERMS

1. Goods
2. Component parts
3. Durable goods
4. Convenience product
5. Specialty product
6. Innovation
7. Continuous innovation
8. Discontinuous innovation
9. Diffusion
10. Innovators
11. Early majority
12. Laggards
13. Equipment
14. Processed materials
15. Raw materials

MULTIPLE CHOICE

1. c
2. d
3. a
4. b
5. c
6. d
7. a
8. b
9. d
10. c
11. b
12. a
13. c
14. b
15. d

CHAPTER IN REVIEW - WRITING TO LEARN

1. A product may be a tangible physical good or an intangible service or idea. The core product is the basic product category benefits and customized benefit(s) the product provides. The actual product is the physical good or delivered service including the packaging and brand name. The augmented product includes both the actual product and any supplementary services such as warranty, credit, delivery, installation, etc.

2. *Convenience* products are purchased frequently with little effort. *Shopping* products are bought only after customers carefully gather information and compare different brands on their attributes and/or price. *Specialty* products have unique characteristics and are important to the buyer. Customers have little interest in unsought products until a need arises.

3. Five product characteristics that have an important effect on how quick (or if) a new product will be adopted by consumers are 1) *relative advantage*, a product ability to provide important benefits; 2) *compatibility* with a consumer's normal way of doing things; 3) product *complexity*, 4) *trialability* or the ability to sample or try out a new product; and 5) product *observability*, the likelihood that other people will see the new product.

A CASE ANALYSIS EXERCISE

1. Mr. Smith has extensive new product experience in national and international product launches.

2. Mr. Smith earned a bachelor of science degree in marketing from the University of Connecticut as well as a master of business administrative degree from the University of Texas.

3. William Smith has worked for the Eastman Kodak Company since 1991, most recently as category manager and director of worldwide marketing for the Advanced Photo System.

4. Mr. Smith has held other Kodak assignments that have included the director of strategic planning and director of marketing.

5. Prior to joining Eastman Kodak, Mr. Smith held key marketing positions at Sterling Drug Corporation and Bristol-Myers.

CHAPTER 10

PRODUCT MANAGEMENT

CHAPTER OVERVIEW

In this chapter, we first learned about some of the different product strategies a firm may choose. Product objectives support broader marketing objectives of a firm and ideally, focus on customer needs. Objectives for individual products may be related to introducing the product, rejuvenating an existing product, or harvesting a declining product. Other strategies focus on entire product lines, different product items which satisfy the same customer need. Marketers may determine that the best strategy is to extend the product line with an upward stretch, a downward stretch, or a two-way stretch. In other cases, objectives relate to a firm's product mix or the product quality.

One way that firms manage existing products is with a brand manager structure where individual brand managers supervise all the marketing activities for a single brand. New products are sometimes both created and managed by entrepreneurs, however, large firms often give new product responsibilities to new product managers who develop marketing for the many different new products the firm develops. In other cases, new products are managed by venture teams. Managing an existing product requires understanding its status in the product life cycle--whether it is the introductory, growth, maturity, or decline stage.

Next, we reviewed how branding creates product identity and the types of branding strategies. A brand is a name, logo, trade character or some other recognizable element that is used to identify or position a product or to convey product attributes. Brands are important because they help in developing and maintaining customer loyalty and help to create value or brand equity. Different categories of brands include brand extensions, family brands, national or manufacturer brands, and private label or store brands. Types of branding strategies include licensing agreements and co-branding strategies.

Finally, packaging and labeling play an important part in developing effective product strategies. Package design communicates a product's identity, benefits, and other important product information. Package labeling in the U.S. is controlled by a number of federal laws aimed at making package labels more helpful to consumers.

CHAPTER OBJECTIVES

1. Explain some of the different product objectives and strategies a firm may choose.

2. Explain how firms manage products throughout the product life cycle.

3. Discuss how branding creates product identity and describe different types of branding strategies.

4. Explain the important part packaging and labeling play in developing effective product strategies.

5. Describe how organizations are structured for new and existing product management.

CHAPTER OUTLINE
Please refer to your textbook in order to define, list, and/or describe the missing parts of the chapter outline. The page numbers given will help guide you through this learning process.

I. CHIPPING AWAY AT THE COMPETITION: CREATING AND NURTURING QUALITY PRODUCTS _____ *(p.261)*

II. USING PRODUCT OBJECTIVES TO DECIDE ON A PRODUCT STRATEGY _____ *(P.261)*
   A. Objectives And Strategies For Individual Products_____ *(p.262)*
   B. Objectives And Strategies For Multiple Products
      1. Product Line Strategies _____ *(p.262)*
         Full-Line Strategy _____ *(p.263)*
         Limited-Line Strategy _____ *(p.263)*
         Stretching The Firm's Product Line _____ *(p.264)*
         Cannibalization _____ *(p.265)*
         Product Mix _____ *(p.265)*
   C. Quality As A Product Objective _____ *(p.265)*

II. MARKETING THROUGHOUT THE PRODUCT LIFE CYCLE _____ *(p.266)*
   A. The Introduction Stage _____ *(p.266)*
   B. The Growth Stage _____ *(p.268)*
   C. The Maturity Stage _____ *(p.268)*
   D. The Decline Stage _____ *(p.268)*

III. CREATING PRODUCT IDENTITY: BRANDING DECISIONS
    A.   What's In A Name (Or A Symbol)?
        Brand _____ (p.270)
        1.   Choosing A Brand Name, Mark, Or Character ____
                _____ (p.271)
        2.   Trademarks _____ (p.272)
    B.   The Importance Of Branding
        Brand Equity _____ (p.273)
        Brand Extension _____ (p.273)
    C.   Branding Strategies
        1.   Individual Brands Versus Family Brands
                Individual Brand Strategy _____ (p.273)
                Family Brand _____ (p.273)
        2.   National and Store Brands
                National or Manufacturer Brands_____
                _____ (p.274)
                Store or Private-Label Brands_____
                _____ (p.274)
        3.   Licensing_____ (p.274)
        4.   Co-Branding_____ (p.275)

V.   CREATING PRODUCT IDENTITY: PACKAGING AND LABELING DECISIONS
    A.   Packaging Functions
        Package _____ (p.276)
    B.   Designing Effective Packaging _____
        _____ (p.277)
    C.   Labeling Regulations_____ (p.277)

VI. ORGANIZING FOR EFFECTIVE PRODUCT MANAGEMENT
    A.   Management Of Existing Products _____
        _____ (p.278)
        1.   Brand Manager _____ (p.278)
        2.   Product Category Manager _____ (p.278)
        3.   Market Manager _____ (p.279)
    B.   Organizing For New-Product Development ____
        _____ (p.279)
        Venture Teams _____
        _____ (p.279)

CHAPTER 10

KEY TERMS

Select the correct term for each definition and write it in the space provided.

Venture teams
Trademark
Brand Manager
Green Packaging
Product life cycle
Cannibalization
National or manufacturer brands
Brand

Brand equity
Product line
Brand extensions
Market manager
Growth stage
Licensing
Product mix

1. _____ A firm's total product offering designed to satisfy a single need or desire of target customers. *(p.262)*

2. _____ The loss of sales of an existing product when a new item in a product line or product family is introduced. *(p.264)*

3. _____ The total set of all products offered for sale by a firm--including all product lines sold to all customer groups. *(p.265)*

4. _____ An individual who is responsible for developing and implementing the marketing plan for a single brand *(p.278)*

5. _____ An individual who is responsible for developing and implementing the marketing plans for products sold to a particular customer group. *(p.279)*

6. _____ A group of people within an organization who work together focusing exclusively on the development of a new product. *(p.279)*

7. _____ The concept that explains how products go through four distinct stages from birth to death: introduction, growth, maturity, and decline. *(p.266)*

8. _____   Price competition may develop during this stage of the product life cycle while driving profits down. *(p.268)*

9. _____   A name, a term, a symbol, or any other unique element of a product that identifies one firm's product(s) and sets them apart from the competition. *(p.270)*

10. _____   The legal name for a brand name, brand mark, or trade character; trademarks may be legally registered by a government, thus obtaining protection for exclusive use in that country. *(p.272)*

11. _____   Packaging that is less harmful to the environment than traditional materials. *(p.277)*

12. _____   The value of a brand related to the brand's ability to reliably attract future customers. *(p.273)*

13. _____   New products which are marketed with the brand name of existing products, often in a different product category. *(p.273)*

14. _____   Brands that are owned by the manufacturer of the product. *(p.274)*

15. _____   Agreement in which one firm sells another firm the right to use a brand name for a specific purpose and for a specific period of time. *(p.274)*

MULTIPLE CHOICE
Identify the most correct answer.

1. In some cases, when the existing product line is quite limited, line items are added at both the upper and lower ends, which is a product strategy called a(n): *(p.264)*
   a. downward line stretch.
   b. upward line stretch.
   c. two-way stretch.
   d. filling out strategy.

2. The length of the product mix refers to: *(p.265)*
    a. the total number of different product items including all of the items in each product line.
    b. the number of different versions of each product.
    c. how closely related the items are in terms of technology, end use, channels of distribution, price range, or customer market.
    d. the number of different products produced by the firm.

3. An individual who is responsible for developing and implementing the marketing plan for all of the brands and products within a product category is a: *(p.278)*
    a. brand manager.
    b. product line manager.
    c. market manager.
    d. product category manager.

4. An individual who is responsible for developing and implementing the marketing plans for products sold to a particular customer group is a: *(p.279)*
    a. market manager.
    b. product group manager.
    c. target manager.
    d. product line manager.

5. A venture team is: *(p.279)*
    a. a business formed by two or more companies that agree to pool certain resources for some common purpose.
    b. a group of people within an organization who work together focusing exclusively on the development of a new product.
    c. a business formed to introduce products into international markets.
    d. a business formed by two or more companies for the purpose of developing new products that will benefit both firms.

6. A product mix: *(p.265)*
    a. involves actually designing the product and planning how it will be manufactured.
    b. means getting individual consumers or organizations that are likely to be future customers to participate in evaluating product benefits during the development stage.
    c. means the total set of all products a firm offers for sale.
    d. none of the above.

7. The process of introducing a product by implementing a complete marketing program is called: *(p.279)*
   a. a product launch.
   b. beta testing.
   c. simulated market testing.
   d. selected consumer testing.

8. A good brand name fits: *(p.271)*
   a. the target market.
   b. the product's benefits and the customer's culture.
   c. legal requirements.
   d. all of the above.

9. A form of repeat purchasing behavior based on a conscious decision to continue buying a product with a particular brand or trademark is: *(p.273)*
   a. inertia.
   b. brand loyalty.
   c. brand extension.
   d. brand equity.

10. A brand that is shared by a group of individual products or individual brands is a(n): *(p.273)*
    a. extended brand.
    b. power brand.
    c. family brand.
    d. national brand.

11. A family brand: *(p.273)*
    a. is shared by a group of individual products or individual brands.
    b. appeals to a narrow segment of the market.
    c. provides customized benefits that uniquely satisfy consumers.
    d. all of the above.

12. Brands that are owned by the manufacturer of the product. *(p.274)*
    a. powerless brands.
    b. segmented brands.
    c. national or manufacturer brands.
    d. private brands.

13. Brands that are owned and sold by a certain retailer or distributor are: *(p.274)*
    a. national brands.
    b. store or private-label brands.
    c. manufacturer brands.
    d. niche brands.

14. Co-branding: *(p.275)*
    a. is an agreement between two brands to work together in marketing a new product.
    b. benefits both partners by providing greater recognition power.
    c. allows for the split of advertising and trade promotion costs.
    d. all of the above.

15. The covering or container for a product which provides product protection, facilitates product use and storage, and supplies important marketing communication is the: *(p.276)*
    a. brown wrapper.
    b. package.
    c. universal product code.
    d. product label.

CHAPTER IN REVIEW - WRITING TO LEARN

1. Explain how product quality is addressed as a product objective.

_____

_____

_____

2. Describe how products are managed throughout their life cycle.

_____

_____

_____

3. Identify the important criteria to be considered in choosing a brand name.

_____

_____

_____

A Case Analysis Exercise

Real People, Real Choices: Meet Dennis Carter, A Decision Maker at Intel

Reread the Opening Vignette on page 260 of your text and answer the following questions.

1. What is significant concerning the product decisions that are made by Dennis Carter?

2. Describe the job title and responsibilities held by Dennis Carter.

3. What product design experience does Dennis Carter offer the Intel Corporation?

4. Identify the names of the corporations using Intel microprocessors.

5. When did Mr. Carter join the Intel Corporation? What were his original responsibilities?

ANSWERS
CHAPTER OUTLINE

I.   CHIPPING AWAY AT THE COMPETITION: CREATING AND NURTURING QUALITY PRODUCTS--Product planning plays a big role in the firm's tactical marketing plans.

II.   USING PRODUCT OBJECTIVES TO DECIDE ON A PRODUCT STRATEGY-- Product objectives provide focus and direction.
   A.   Objectives And Strategies For Individual Products--For new products, the objectives relate to successful introduction.   For mature products, the objectives may focus on breathing new life into a product.
   B.   Objectives And Strategies For Multiple Products
      1.   Product Line Strategies--A firm's total product offering designed to satisfy a single need or desire of target customers.
         Full-Line Strategy--A large number of variations in a firm's product line.
         Limited-Line Strategy--A firm that markets a smaller number of product variations.
         Stretching The Firm's Product Line--An upward line stretch, a downward line stretch, a two-way stretch, a filling-out strategy, and contracting a product line strategy.
         Cannibalization--The loss of sales of an existing

product when a new item in a product line or product family is introduced.
Product Mix--The set of all products a firm offers for sale.
C. Quality As A Product Objective--Product quality objectives coincide with marketing objectives.

III. MARKETING THROUGHOUT THE PRODUCT LIFE CYCLE--The concept that explains how products go through four distinct stages from birth to death: introduction, growth, maturity, and decline.
A. The Introduction Stage--The first stage of the product life cycle in which slow growth follows the introduction of a new product in the marketplace.
B. The Growth Stage--The second stage in the product life cycle during which the product is accepted and sales rapidly increase.
C. The Maturity Stage--The third and longest stage in the product life cycle in which sales peak and profit margins narrow.
D. The Decline Stage--The final stage in the product life cycle in which sales decrease as customer needs change.

III. CREATING PRODUCT IDENTITY: BRANDING DECISIONS
A. What's In a Name (or a Symbol)?
Brand--A name, a term, a symbol, or any other unique element of a product that identifies one firm's product(s) and sets them apart from the competition.
1. Choosing a Brand Name, Mark, or Character--A good brand is: easy to say, spell, read, and remember. The name should also fit the target market, fit the product's benefits, fit the customer's culture, and fit legal requirements.
2. Trademarks--The legal term for a brand name, brand mark, or trade character; trademarks may be legally registered by a government, thus obtaining protection for exclusive use in that country.
B. The Importance of Branding
Brand Equity--The value of a brand to an organization.
Brand Extension--A new product sold with the same brand name as a strong existing brand.
C. Branding Strategies
1. Individual Brands Versus Family Brands
Individual Brand Strategy--A separate, unique brand for each product item.
Family Brand--A brand that is shared by a group of individual products or individual brands.
2. National and Store Brands
National or Manufacturer Brands--Brands that are owned by the manufacturer of the product.
Store or Private Label Brands--Brands that are owned and sold by a certain retailer or distributor.

3. Licensing--An agreement in which one firm sells another firm the right to use a brand name for a specific purpose and for a specific period of time.
4. Co-Branding--An agreement between two brands to work together in marketing a new product.

V. CREATING PRODUCT IDENTITY: PACKAGING AND LABELING DECISIONS
   A. Packaging Functions
      Package--The covering or container for a product which provides product protection, facilitates product use and storage, and supplies important marketing communication.
   B. Designing Effective Packaging--Packaging material, (Green packaging), Packaging shape, size, etc.
   C. Labeling Regulations--The Federal Fair Packaging and Labeling Act of 1966 controls package communications and labeling in the United States.

VI. ORGANIZING FOR EFFECTIVE PRODUCT MANAGEMENT
   A. Management Of Existing Products--Product management may include brand managers, product category managers, and market managers.
      1. Brand Managers--An individual who is responsible for developing and implementing the marketing plan for a single brand.
      2. Product Category Manager--An individual who is responsible for developing and implementing the marketing plan for all of the brands and products within a product category.
      3. Market Manager--An individual who is responsible for developing and implementing the marketing plans for products sold to a particular customer group.
   B. Organizing For New-Product Development--Often individuals who are assigned to manage new-product development are especially creative people with entrepreneurial skills.
      Venture Teams--Groups of people within an organization who work together focusing exclusively on the development of a new product.

CHAPTER 10
ANSWERS

KEY TERMS	MULTIPLE CHOICE

1. Product line	1.	c
2. Cannibalization	2.	a
3. Product mix	3.	d
4. Brand manager	4.	a
5. Market manager	5.	b
6. Venture teams	6.	c
7. Product life cycle	7.	a
8. Growth stage	8.	d
9. Brand	9.	b
10. Trademark	10.	c
11. Green packaging	11.	a
12. Brand equity	12.	c
13. Brand extensions	13.	b
14. National or manufacturer brands	14.	d
15. Licensing	15.	b

CHAPTER IN REVIEW - WRITING TO LEARN

1. Product objectives often address product quality or the ability of the product to satisfy customers. Product quality is tied to customer expectations of product performance. For individual products, quality may mean durability, degree of precision, ease of use and repair, or degree of aesthetic pleasure. Product quality objectives are likely to focus on the level and the consistency of product quality.

2. In the introductory stage, the goal is to get customers to try the product. During growth, firms focus on establishing brand loyalty and may improve the product. In maturity, significant product modification may occur and new users may be attracted with market differentiation strategies. During the decline stage, firms must decide whether to keep the product or to phase it out.

3. Brand names may be easy to say, spell, read and remember and should fit the target market, the product's benefits, the customer's culture, and legal requirements.

A CASE ANALYSIS EXERCISE

1. Dennis Carter makes product decisions that affect the "brains" of most of the personal computers manufactured in the world, very possibly including your own.

2. As a Vice President and General Manager of Corporate Marketing at Intel Corporation, he is responsible for Intel's marketing communications, advertising, public relations, and corporate and end-user marketing programs.

3. Mr. Carter worked as an Engineering Manager for Rockwell International.

4. Intel makes the microprocessors that power personal computers made by IBM, Compaq, Dell and many other computer industry giants.

5. Mr. Carter joined Intel in 1981 as Product Marketing Engineer and Software Marketing Engineer.

CHAPTER 11

BROADENING THE PRODUCT FOCUS:
MARKETING INTANGIBLES AND SERVICES

CHAPTER OVERVIEW

The purpose of this chapter is to describe the characteristics of services and explain marketing of intangibles. Important service characteristics include intangibility (they cannot be seen, touched, or smelled), perishability (they cannot be stored), variability (they are never exactly the same), and inseparability from the product (most services are produced, sold, and consumed at the same time.

The satisfaction of service customers, that is, the perception of service quality, is related to prior expectations and can be measured by gap analysis or critical incident technique. In developing strategies for services, marketers focus on both the core service--the basic benefit received from the service--and on augmented services--innovative features, and the unique delivery systems, etc. Sometimes marketing intangibles means packaging, promoting, and selling people such as politicians and celebrities as well as the promotion of causes and ideas, known as cause marketing.

Finally, in marketing intangibles, some important marketing mix elements such as packaging and labeling are not relevant. Price is very important in services marketing as an indicator of quality. Promotion, as with the marketing of goods, must focus on different market segments.

CHAPTER OBJECTIVES

1. Explain the marketing of people, places, and ideas.

2. Describe the four characteristics of services, and understand how services differ from goods.

3. Explain how marketers measure service quality.

4. Explain marketing strategies for services and not-for-profit organizations.

CHAPTER OUTLINE

Please refer to your textbook in order to define, list, and/or describe the missing parts of the chapter outline. The page numbers given will help guide you through this learning process.

I. MARKETING WHAT ISN'T THERE
    Intangibles _____ (p.286)
    A. Does Marketing Work For Intangibles? _____
        _____ (p.287)
        1. Mission Statement _____ (p.288)
        2. Situation Analysis _____ (p.288)
        3. Product Life Cycle _____ (p.288)
    B. Marketing People, Places, And Ideas
        1. Marketing People
            Pure Selling Approach _____ (p.289)
            Product Improvement Approach _____
            _____ (p.289)
            Market Fulfillment Approach _____ (p.289)
        2. Marketing Places _____ (p.289)
        3. Marketing Ideas
            Idea Marketing _____
            _____ (p.290)
            Cause Marketing _____
            _____ (p.291)

II. WHAT IS A SERVICE?
    Services _____ (p.293)
    A. Characteristics of Services
        1. Intangibility _____ (p.293)
        2. Perishability _____ (p.293)
            Capacity Management _____ (p.293)
        3. Variability _____ (p.293)
        4. Inseparability _____ (p.294)
            Service Encounter _____ (p.294)
            Disintermediation _____ (p.294)
    B. The Goods/Services Continuum _____
        _____ (p.294)
        1. Good-Dominated Products
            Embodying _____ (p.294)
        2. Equipment- or Facility-Based Services
            Facility-driven services _____ (p.296)
            Operational Factors _____ (p.296)
            Locational Factors _____ (p.296)
            Environmental Factors _____ (p.296)
        3. People-Based Services _____ (p.296)
    C. Core And Augmented Services
        Core Service _____ (p.296)
        Augmented Services _____ (p.297)

III. PROVIDING QUALITY SERVICE
    A. Judging Service Quality _____
        _____ (p.299)

      1.   Quality is About Exceeding Expectations
           Internal Marketing _____
           _____ (p.300)
      2.   Evaluative Dimensions Of Service Quality
           Search Qualities _____ (p.301)
           Experience Qualities _____ (p.301)
           Credence Qualities _____ (p.301)
   B.   Measuring Service Quality
      1.   Gap Analysis_____ (p.302)
      2.   The Critical Incident Technique_____ (p.303)

IV. STRATEGIES FOR DEVELOPING AND MANAGING SERVICES
   A.   Services As Theater _____ (p.303)
   B.   Targeting And Positioning Strategies For Services
      1.   Targeting: Defining the Service Customer
           or Audience
           Audience Maintenance _____ (p.306)
           Audience Enrichment _____ (p.306)
           Audience Expansion _____ (p.306)
           Audience Development _____ (p.306)
      2.   Positioning: Defining the Service to
           Customers
           Tangibles _____ (p.306)
           Physical Evidence _____ (p.306)
           Responsiveness _____ (p.306)
           Empathy _____ (p.306)
           Assurance _____ (p.307)

CHAPTER 11

KEY TERMS

Select the correct term for each definition and write it in the space provided.

Augmented services
Core service
Empathy
Embodying
Services
Physical evidence
Standardized service
Internal marketing

Gap analysis
Service encounter
Capacity management
Idea marketing
Disintermediation
Critical incident technique
Cause marketing

1. _____ Products that are intangible and which are exchanged directly from producer to customer. (p.293)

2. _____ The actual interaction between the customer and the service provider. (p.294)

3. _____ Marketing activities aimed at employees in an effort to inform them about the firm's offerings and their high quality. *(p.300)*

4. _____ A marketing research methodology that measures the difference between a customer's expectation of service quality and what actually occurred. *(p.302)*

5. _____ A method of measuring service quality in which customer complaints are used to identify critical incidents, specific face-to-face contacts between consumers and service providers that cause problems and lead to dissatisfaction. *(p.303)*

6. _____ The basic benefit that is obtained as a result of having a service performed. *(p.296)*

7. _____ The core service plus additional services provided to enhance its value. *(p.297)*

8. _____ The process of eliminating interaction between customers and salespeople. *(p.294)*

9. _____ A service which is designed and delivered in a manner in which every customer receives almost exactly the same outcome or product. *(p.293)*

10. _____ The inclusion of a service with a purchase of a physical good. *(p.294)*

11. _____ Marketing activities that seek to gain market share for a concept, philosophy, belief, or issue. *(p.290)*

12. _____ A visible signal that communicates not only a product's quality but also the product's desired market position to the consumer. *(p.306)*

13. _____ The process by which the offering is adjusted in an attempt to match demand. *(p.293)*

14. _____ An organization that says it understands its customers' needs and genuinely cares about their welfare expresses: *(p.306)*

15. _____ Marketing activities in which firms seek to have their corporate identity linked to a good cause through advertising, public service, and publicity. *(p.291)*

MULTIPLE CHOICE
Identify the most correct answer.

1. All services share the following characteristics that make them distinct from physical products: *(p.293)*
    a. Intangibility, perishability, inseparability, and variability.
    b. Tangibility, inseparability, variability, and durability.
    c. Tangibility, perishability, durability, and variability.
    d. Intangibility, perishability, inseparability, and durability.

2. Service intangibility means that: *(p.293)*
    a. services can't be stored.
    b. the same service activities are performed in different ways from one day to the next.
    c. customers can't see, touch, or smell good service.
    d. both the customer and the service provider must be present at the same time for the service to be delivered.

3. The strategy of including a service with the sale of a physical good is termed: *(p.294)*
    a. service continuum.
    b. embodying.
    c. variability.
    d. resourcing.

4. Facility-driven services, such as automatic car washes, amusement parks, museums, movie theaters, health clubs, tanning salons, and zoos, must be concerned with the following important factors: *(p.296)*
    a. Operational factors.
    b. Locational factors.
    c. Environmental factors.
    d. All of the above.

5. Search qualities that a customer can use to choose among products refer to: *(p.301)*
   a. product characteristics that can only be determined during or after consumption.
   b. attributes that are difficult to evaluate even after we've experienced them.
   c. attributes that the consumer can examine prior to purchase.
   d. techniques that can be used to provide insights on service satisfaction.

6. Some major gaps identified during gap analysis include: *(p.302)*
   a. Management understands what the customer's expectations are.
   b. Management fails to establish a quality control program.
   c. Employees deliver the service at the level specified by the company.
   d. All of the above.

7. Specific face-to-face contacts between consumers and service providers that cause problems and lead to dissatisfaction are called: *(p.303)*
   a. critical incidents.
   b. unreasonable demands.
   c. unrealistic expectations.
   d. cause marketing.

8. An example of augmented services that an airline may offer is: *(p.297)*
   a. safe transportation from point A to point B.
   b. frequent flyer miles.
   c. arriving intact at your destination.
   d. none the above.

9. Marketers whose primary offerings are experience-based products that cannot be touched are: *(p.286)*
   a. standardized services.
   b. tangibles.
   c. intangibles.
   d. tangible services.

10. Many companies feel that the best way to bring about social change is through: *(p.291)*
    a. idea marketing.
    b. theory marketing.
    c. influence marketing.
    d. cause marketing.

11. An example from the back stage region of a service performance for a fancy restaurant is: *(p.303)*
    a. appropriate music playing softly in the background.
    b. the kitchen where the food is prepared.
    c. tables that are clean and elegantly set.
    d. flaming delicacies brought to the table.

12. Idea marketing seeks to gain market share for a: *(p.290)*
    a. concept, philosophy, belief, or issue.
    b. theory, belief, view, or opinion.
    c. philosophy, theory, opinion, or belief.
    d. issue, opinion, theory, or belief.

13. The electric company knowing that demand for its service will rise systematically as the temperature goes up, is an example of: *(p.293)*
    a. demand management.
    b. standardized service.
    c. capacity management.
    d. cause marketing.

14. Organizations try to attract visitors (and their dollars) to a site, whether a resort, theme park, or city, by engaging in: *(p.289)*
    a. tourism marketing.
    b. organization marketing.
    c. target marketing.
    d. brand marketing.

15. Like other products, celebrities even rename themselves to craft a: *(p.289)*
    a. "market target".
    b. "brand target".
    c. "brand market".
    d. "brand identity".

CHAPTER IN REVIEW - WRITING TO LEARN

1. Describe the characteristics of services.

_____

_____

_____

2. Explain how marketers evaluate service quality.

_____

_____

_____

3. Explain the marketing of nonprofit organizations.

_____

_____

_____

A Case Analysis Exercise

Real People, Real Choices: Meet Charles Waddell, A Decision Maker at the Carolina Panthers

Reread the Opening Vignette on page 286 of your text and answer the following questions.

1. What position is held by Charles Waddell at the Carolina Panthers?

2. What are Charles Waddell's responsibilities at the Carolina Panthers?

3. Describe the experience gained by Charles Waddell prior to accepting the position as the director of marketing.

4. Identify the marketing activities that are carried out during the off-season by Charles Waddell.

5. Where did Charles Waddell earn his undergraduate degree?

ANSWERS
CHAPTER OUTLINE

I. MARKETING WHAT ISN'T THERE
   Intangibles--Experience-based products that cannot be touched.
   A. Does Marketing Work for Intangibles?--Yes, if the basics of developing a strategic plan are applied.
      1. Mission Statement--Should include concrete goals.
      2. Situation Analysis--An assessment of environmental threats and opportunities.

3. Product Life Cycle--The organization's goals must consider which part of the product life cycle it is in.
    B. Marketing People, Places, and Ideas
        1. Marketing People
            Pure Selling Approach--The agent presents a client's qualifications to potential "buyers" until he or she finds one who is willing to act as an intermediary.
            Product Improvement Approach--The agent works with the client to modify certain characteristics that will increase market value.
            Market Fulfillment Approach--The agent scans the market to identify unmet needs.
        2. Marketing Places--In tourism marketing, organizations try to attract visitors (and their dollars) to a site, resort, theme park, or city.
        3. Marketing Ideas
            Idea Marketing – Marketing activities that seek to gain market share for a concept, philosophy, belief, or issue by using elements of the marketing mix to create or change a target market's attitude or behavior.
            Cause Marketing--Marketing activities in which firms seek to have their corporate identity linked to a good cause through advertising, public service, and publicity.

II. WHAT IS A SERVICE?
    Services--Intangible products that are exchanged directly from producer to the customer.
    A. Characteristics of Services
        1. Intangibility--Customers can't see, touch, or smell good service.
        2. Perishability--Firms can't store its services, use it or lose it.
            Capacity Management--The process by which the offering is adjusted in an attempt to match demand.
        3. Variability--The inevitable differences in a service provider's performance from one day to the next.
        4. Inseparability--A service can only take place at the time the service provider performs an act on either the customer or the customer's possession.
            Service Encounter--The actual interaction between the customer and the service provider.
            Disintermediation--The process of eliminating interaction between customers and salespeople.
    B. The Goods/Services Continuum--Most products are a combination of goods and services.
        1. Good-Dominated Products Embodying--The inclusion of a service with a purchase of a physical good.

2. Equipment- Or Facility-Based Services
Facility-driven services--Include three important factors that must be considered.
Operational Factors---Technologies that show customers how to use service as well as move them smoothly through it.
Locational Factors---How far the service is from purchasers.
Environmental Factors--Creation of an attractive environment to lure customers into the market.
3. People-Based Services--Please people with less and less time to perform various tasks.
C. Core And Augmented Services
Core Service--The basic benefit that is obtained as a result of having a service performed.
Augmented Services--The core service plus additional services provided to enhance value.

III. PROVIDING QUALITY SERVICE
A. Judging Service Quality--Satisfaction or dissatisfaction is more than a reaction to the actual performance quality.
1. Quality is About Exceeding Expectations
Internal Marketing--Marketing activities aimed at employees in an effort to inform them about the firm's offerings and their high quality.
2. Evaluative Dimensions Of Service Quality
Search Qualities--The attributes that the consumer can examine prior to purchase
Experience Qualities--Product characteristics that customers can determine during or after consumption.
Credence Qualities--Attributes we find difficult to evaluate even after we've experienced them.
B. Measuring Service Quality
1. Gap Analysis--A marketing methodology that measures the difference between a customer's expectation of service quality and what actually occurred.
2. The Critical Incident Technique--A method for measuring service quality in which customer complaints are used to identify critical incidents, specific face-to-face contacts between consumers and service providers that cause problems and lead to dissatisfaction.

IV. STRATEGIES FOR DEVELOPING AND MANAGING SERVICES
A. Services As Theater--A service performance often takes place in two areas, the back stage and the front stage.

B.   Targeting And Positioning Strategies For Services
      1.   Targeting: Defining The Service Customer Or
            Audience.
            Audience Maintenance--Goal is to deepen their
            commitment to the organization.
            Audience Enrichment--Goal is to enhance the
            experience of attendees to ensure their ongoing
            loyalty to the organization.
            Audience Expansion--Goal is to increase the number
            of people who attend.
            Audience Development--Goal is to convince non-
            attenders that they would enjoy.
      2.   Positioning: Defining The Service To Customers
            Tangibles--Services often rely heavily on physical
            evidence.
            Physical   Evidence--A   visible   signal   that
            communicates not only a product's quality, but also
            the product's desired market position to the
            consumer.
            Responsiveness--Speed and care with which they
            respond to customers requests.
            Empathy--Organization   understands   a   customer's
            needs and genuinely cares about their welfare.
            Assurance--Knowledge or competence of it's
            employees.

CHAPTER 11
ANSWERS

KEY TERMS   ## MULTIPLE CHOICE

 1. Services   1. a
 2. Service encounter   2. c
 3. Internal marketing   3. b
 4. Gap analysis   4. d
 5. Critical incident technique   5. c
 6. Core service   6. b
 7. Augmented services   7. a
 8. Disintermediation   8. b
 9. Standardized service   9. c
10. Embodying   10. d
11. Idea marketing   11. b
12. Physical evidence   12. a
13. Capacity management   13. c
14. Empathy   14. a
15. Cause marketing   15. d

CHAPTER IN REVIEW - WRITING TO LEARN

1. Important service characteristics include 1) intangibility (they cannot be seen, or touched, or smelled), 2) perishability (they cannot be stored), 3) variability (they are never <u>exactly</u> the same) and 4) inseparability from the producer (most services are produced, sold, and consumed at the same time).

2. Both qualitative and quantitative research methods may be used to measure customer satisfaction. Gap analysis measures the difference between customer expectations of service quality and what actually occurred. Using a critical incident technique, service firms can identify the specific contacts between customers and service providers which create dissatisfaction.

3. Non-profit organizations also develop marketing strategies to "sell" social services, cultural experiences, ideas such as environmental protection, or a political or religious philosophy.

A CASE ANALYSIS EXERCISE

1. Charles Waddell is director of marketing and sponsorships for the Carolina Panthers of the National Football League.

2. Charles Waddell is responsible for the coordination of the Panthers sponsorship packages and team advertising.

3. In addition to his experience as a football player, Charles Waddell served as assistant commissioner of the Big Ten Conference, where he focused on league licensing and marketing. Prior to joining the Big Ten, Waddell was a vice president of NCNB Capital Markets in Charlotte.

4. Although the team works hardest in the fall, Waddell is hard at work in the off-season, as this is the time to prospect new sponsors, sell advertising rights, and create new sponsorship proposals.

5. Charles Waddell graduated with honors from the University of North Carolina in 1975 with a bachelor of science degree in industrial relations.

CHAPTER 12

PRICING THE PRODUCT

CHAPTER OVERVIEW

In this chapter, we learned the importance of pricing. Price, the amount of outlay of money, goods, services or deeds given in exchange for a product, may be monetary such as dues and rent or nonmonetary such as a vote for a candidate and contribution for time.

Demand is the amount of a product customers are willing to buy at different prices. Price elasticity of demand is the sensitivity of customers to changing prices. With elastic demand, changes in price create large changes in demand while when demand is inelastic, increases in price have little effect on demand so that total revenue increases.

Break-even analysis uses fixed and variable costs to identify how many units will have to be sold at a certain price in order to begin making a profit. Marginal analysis uses both costs and estimates of product demand to identify the price that will maximize profits.

Finally, like other elements of the marketing mix, pricing is influenced by a variety of external environmental factors. This includes economic trends such as inflation and recession, and the firm's competitive environment. That is, whether the firm does business in an oligopoly, a monopoly, or a more competitive environment.

CHAPTER OBJECTIVES

1. Explain the importance of pricing and how prices can take both monetary and nonmonetary forms.

2. Understand the pricing objectives that marketers typically have in planning pricing strategies.

3. Describe how customer demand influences pricing decisions.

4. Describe how marketers use costs, demands, and revenue to make pricing decisions.

5. Understand some of the environmental factors that affect pricing strategies.

CHAPTER OUTLINE

Please refer to your textbook in order to define, list, and/or describe the missing parts of the chapter outline. The page numbers given will help guide you through this learning process.

I. "YES, BUT WHAT DOES IT COST?"
    A. Monetary and Nonmonetary Prices
        Price _____ (p.318)
        Bartering _____ (p.319)
        Opportunity Cost _____ (p.319)
        Cost-Value Relationship _____ (p.319)
    B. The Importance of Pricing Decisions _____
        _____ (p.320)
    C. Pricing and the Marketing Mix
        1. Price and Place _____ (p.320)
        2. Price and Product _____ (p.321)
        3. Price and Promotion _____ (p.322)

II. DEVELOPING PRICING OBJECTIVES _____
    _____ (p.322)
    A. Sales or Market Share Objectives _____
    _____ (p.324)
    B. Profit Objectives _____ (p.324)
    C. Competitive Effect Objectives _____
    _____ (p.324)
    D. Customer Satisfaction Objectives _____
    _____ (p.324)
    E. Image Enhancement Objectives _____
    _____ (p.325)
    F. Flexibility of Price Objectives _____
    _____ (p.325)

III. ESTIMATING DEMAND: HOW DEMAND INFLUENCES PRICING _____
    _____ (p.325)
    A. Demand Curves _____ (p.325)
        Law of Demand _____ (p.326)
        1. Shifts in Demand _____ (p.326)
        2. Estimating Demand _____ (p.327)
    B. The Price Elasticity of Demand _____ (p.328)
        1. Elastic and Inelastic Demand
        Elastic Demand _____ (p.328)
        Inelastic Demand _____ (p.328)
        2. Influences on Demand Elasticity _____
        _____ (p.330)
        Income Effect _____ (p.330)

IV. DETERMINING COST
    A. Types of Costs _____ (p.332)
        1. Variable Costs _____ (p.333)
        2. Fixed Costs _____ (p.333)
        3. Total Costs _____ (p.334)
    B. Break-Even Analysis _____ (p.334)

C. Marginal Analysis _____ (p.336)
    Marginal Cost _____ (p.336)
    Marginal Revenue _____ (p.336)

V. EVALUATING THE PRICING ENVIRONMENT _____
    _____ (p.338)
    A. The Economy _____ (p.338)
        1. Trimming the Fat: Pricing in a Recession ____
            _____ (p.338)
        2. Increasing Prices: Responding to Inflation ___
            _____ (p.339)
    B. The Competition _____ (p.339)
    C. Consumer Trends _____ (p.340)
    D. International Environmental Influences _____
        _____ (p.341)
        Price Subsidies _____ (p.341)

KEY TERMS

Select the correct term for each definition and write it in the space provided.

Marginal analysis   Price elasticity of demand
Bartering   Inferior goods
Price subsidies   Marginal revenue
Fixed costs   Marginal cost
Price   Total costs
Cross-elasticity of demand   Demand
Substitute   Break-Even Analysis
Variable costs

1. _____   The amount of outlay, i.e., money, goods, services, or deeds, that is given in exchange for a product. *(p.318)*

2. _____   The practice of exchanging a good or service for another good or service of like value. *(p.319)*

3. _____   The amount of a product that customers will be willing to buy at different prices, all other things being equal. *(p.325)*

4. _____   A measure of the sensitivity of customers to changes in price; the percentage change in unit sales that result from a percentage change in price. *(p.328)*

5. _____ The costs of production that are tied to and vary depending on the number of units produced; variable costs typically include raw materials, processed materials, component parts and labor. *(p.333)*

6. _____ Costs of production that do not change with the number of units produced. *(p.333)*

7. _____ The total of the fixed costs and the variable costs for a set number of units produced. *(p.334)*

8. _____ A method for determining the number of units which will have to be produced and sold at a given price to break even, i.e., to neither make a profit nor suffer a loss. *(p.334)*

9. _____ A method of analysis that uses costs and demands to identify the price which will maximize profits. *(p.336)*

10. _____ The increase in total cost that results from producing one additional unit of a product. *(p.336)*

11. _____ When changes in the prices of other products affect the demand for a given item. *(p.332)*

12. _____ For some goods, as your income increases, your demand decreases. *(p.331)*

13. _____ A product that can satisfy the demand of another product. *(p.330)*

14. _____ Government payments made to protect domestic businesses or to reimburse them when they must price at or below cost to make a sale. *(p.341)*

15. _____ The increase in total revenue (income) that results from producing and selling one additional unit of a product. *(p.336)*

MULTIPLE CHOICE
Identify the most correct answer.

1. The value of something that is given up to obtain something else is called: *(p.319)*
   a. bartering.
   b. a cost-value relationship.
   c. a professional fee.
   d. opportunity cost.

2. Marketers often have a very difficult time convincing people that the value they receive is worth the price they have to pay for such products, which is known as the perceived: *(p.319)*
   a. opportunity cost.
   b. cost-value relationship.
   c. barter dollars.
   d. monetary rate.

3. What classification of pricing objectives (and strategies) are tailored to different geographic areas and time periods?
   a. flexibility of price objectives.
   b. image enhancement objectives.
   c. profit objectives.
   d. sales or market share objectives.

4. If prices decrease, customers will buy more, is known as the: *(p.326)*
   a. income effect on demand.
   b. backward-bending demand.
   c. law of demand.
   d. consumer pricing sensitivity.

5. In the simplest terms, price elasticity of demand is calculated as follows: *(p.328)*
   a. Percentage change in price divided by percentage change in quantity.
   b. Percentage change in quantity divided by percentage change in price.
   c. Percentage change in quantity multiplied by percentage change in price.
   d. Percentage change in price subtracted from percentage change in quantity.

6. When a change in price results in a large change in quantity demanded, demand is said to be: *(p.328)*
   a. elastic.
   b. cross-elastic.
   c. inelastic.
   d. fixed.

7. Fixed costs include: *(p.333)*
   a.   raw materials.
   b.   labor.
   c.   rent or the cost of owning and maintaining the factory.
   d.   all of the above.

8. At the break-even point: *(p.334)*
   a.   marketers can identify how many units of a product have to be sold to make money.
   b.   revenue or income from sales are just equal to costs.
   c.   variable costs equal fixed costs.
   d.   none the above.

9. The contribution per unit is calculated as: *(p.335)*
   a.   the total fixed costs divided by the variable costs.
   b.   the difference between the total fixed costs and the variable costs.
   c.   the sum of the total fixed cost and the target profit per unit.
   d.   the difference between what a firm sells a product for (the revenue per unit) and the variable costs.

10. The increase in total revenue (income) that results from producing and selling one additional unit of a product is called: *(p.336)*
   a.   marginal revenue.
   b.   revenue goal.
   c.   marginal cost.
   d.   per-unit profit.

11. When customers are very sensitive to changes in prices, and a change in price results in a substantial change in the quantity demanded, this is called: *(p.328)*
   a.   inelastic demand.
   b.   sensitivity demand.
   c.   quality demand.
   d.   elastic demand.

12. The _____ effect on demand means that changes in your earnings affect demand for a product, even if its price remains the same. *(p.330)*
   a.   substitution.
   b.   price.
   c.   income.
   d.   earnings.

13. For products such as clothing and housing, these are examples of: *(p.331)*
   a.   normal goods.
   b.   inferior goods.
   c.   superior goods.
   d.   staple goods.

14. The increase in total revenue (income) that results from producing and selling one additional unit of a product is: *(p.336)*
   a. marginal analysis.
   b. marginal revenue.
   c. marginal income.
   d. marginal cost.

15. In addition to demand and costs, factors in the firm's _____ environment are important to making successful pricing decisions: *(p.338)*
   a. demand.
   b. international.
   c. internal.
   d. external.

CHAPTER IN REVIEW - WRITING TO LEARN

1. Explain how price can take both monetary and nonmonetary forms.

_____

_____

_____

2. Describe the concept of price elasticity of demand.

_____

_____

_____

3. Describe the pricing objectives that marketers typically have in planning pricing strategies.

_____

_____

_____

A Case Analysis Exercise

Real People, Real Choices: Meet Randall Poindexter, A Decision Maker at Bojangles' Restaurants, Inc.

Reread the Opening Vignette on page 318 of your text and answer the following questions.

1. Where was Bojangles founded? What market does it specialize in serving?

2. Describe Randall Poindexter's job at Bojangles.

3. What are Randall Poindexter's responsibilities at Bojangles?

4. What is the size of the Bojangles' operation?

5. What are Bojangles' key strengths?

ANSWERS
CHAPTER OUTLINE

I. "YES, BUT WHAT DOES IT COST?"
   A. Monetary and Nonmonetary Prices
       Price--The value that customers give up or exchange to obtain a desired product.
       Bartering--The practice of exchanging a good or service for another good or service of like value.
       Opportunity Cost--The value of something that is given up to obtain something else.
       Cost-Value Relationship--The challenges associated with the marketing of people or ideas.
   B. The Importance of Pricing Decisions--Pricing is probably the least understood and least appreciated element of the marketing mix.
   C. Pricing and the Marketing Mix
       1. Price and Place--Pricing decisions must be considered from the viewpoint of each member of the channel of distribution - the manufacturers, wholesalers, and retailers - that help get the product to consumers.
       2. Price and Product--The price of the product must cover the costs of doing business but price also sends a signal about product quality. The stage of the product's life cycle also affects pricing.
       3. Price and Promotion--It is important that the advertising strategies justify the cost of the product.

II. DEVELOPING PRICING OBJECTIVES--Pricing objectives must support the broader objectives of the firm (such as maximizing shareholder value) as well as its overall marketing objectives (such as increasing market share).
   A. Sales or Market Share Objectives--Often the objective of pricing strategy is to maximize sales (in dollars or in units) or to increase market share.
   B. Profit Objectives--A profit objective focuses on a target level of profit growth or a desired net profit margin.
   C. Competitive Effect Objectives--The pricing plan is intended to have a certain effect on the marketing efforts of the competition.
   D. Customer Satisfaction Objectives--Many quality-focused firms believe that profits result from making customer satisfaction the primary objective.
   E. Image Enhancement Objectives--Price is often an important means of communicating not only quality but also image to prospective customers.
   F. Flexibility of Price Objectives--Often it is necessary to develop pricing objectives (and strategies) tailored to different geographic areas and time periods.

III. ESTIMATING DEMAND: HOW DEMAND INFLUENCES PRICING--Demand is customers' desire for products.
   A. Demand Curves--Show the quality of a product that customers will buy in a market during a period of time at various prices if all other factors remain the same.
      The Law of Demand--As the price of the product goes up, the number of units that customers are willing to buy goes down. If price decreases, customers will buy more.
      1. Shifts in Demand--An upward shift in the demand curve means that at any given price, demand is greater than before the shift occurs.
      2. Estimating Demand--All marketing planning and budgeting must be based on reasonably accurate estimates of potential sales.
   B. The Price Elasticity of Demand--The percent change in unit sales that results from a percentage change in price.
      1. Elastic and Inelastic Demand
         Elastic Demand--Customers who are very sensitive to changes in prices, and a change in price results in a substantial change in the quantity demanded.
         Inelastic Demand--A change in price has little or no effect on the quantity that consumers are willing to buy and demand.
      2. Influences on Demand Elasticity--If a product has a close substitute, its demand will be elastic; that is, a change in price will result in a change in demand, as consumers move to buy the substitute product.

Income Effect--Changes in income affect demand for a product, even if its price remains the same.

III. DETERMINING COST
    A.   Types of Costs--How much the price exceeds the costs determines the amount of profit the firm may earn, everything else being equal.
        1.   Variable Costs--The costs of production (raw and processed materials, parts, and labor) that are tied to, and vary depending on, the number of units produced.
        2.   Fixed Costs--Costs of production that do not change with the number of units produced.
        3.   Total Costs--The total of the fixed costs and the variable costs for a set number of units produced.
    B.   Break-Even Analysis--A method for determining the number of units that a firm must produce and sell at a given price to cover all its costs.
    C.   Marginal Analysis--A method that uses cost and demand to identify the price which will maximize profits.
Marginal Cost--The increase in total cost that results from producing one additional unit of a product.
Marginal Revenue--The increase in total revenue (income) that results from producing and selling one additional unit of a product.

IV. EVALUATING THE PRICING ENVIRONMENT--An understanding of the factors in the firm's external environment are important to make successful pricing decisions.
    A.   The Economy--The business cycle, inflation, economic growth, and consumer confidence all help to determine whether one pricing strategy or another will succeed.
        1.   Trimming the Fat: Pricing in a Recession--During recessions, consumers grow more price sensitive.
        2.   Increasing Prices: Responding to Inflation-- Economic trends also influence a firm's ability to increase prices because they affect what consumers see as an acceptable or unacceptable price range for a product.
    B.   The Competition--Decision makers must worry constantly about how the competition will respond to their pricing actions.
    C.   Consumer Trends--Culture and demographics determine how consumers think and behave and so have a large impact on all marketing decisions.
    D.   International Environmental Influences--The currency exchange rate influences pricing decisions by firms.
Price Subsidies--Government payments made to protect domestic businesses or to reimburse them when they must price at or below cost to make a sale. The subsidy can be a cash payment or tax relief.

KEY TERMS	MULTIPLE CHOICE

	KEY TERMS		MULTIPLE CHOICE
1.	Price	1.	d
2.	Bartering	2.	b
3.	Demand	3.	a
4.	Price elasticity of demand	4.	c
5.	Variable costs	5.	b
6.	Fixed costs	6.	a
7.	Total costs	7.	c
8.	Break-even analysis	8.	b
9.	Marginal analysis	9.	d
10.	Marginal cost	10.	a
11.	Cross-elasticity of demand	11.	d
12.	Inferior goods	12.	c
13.	Substitute	13.	a
14.	Price subsidies	14.	b
15.	Marginal revenue	15.	d

CHAPTER IN REVIEW - WRITING TO LEARN

1. Price, the amount of outlay of money, goods, services or deeds given in exchange for a product may be monetary (e.g., dues, tuition, professional fee, rent, donations, etc.) or nonmonetary (e.g., a vote for a candidate, contribution of time or effort).

2. Price elasticity of demand is the sensitivity of customers to changing prices. With elastic demand, changes in price create large changes in demand while when demand is inelastic, increases in price have little effect on demand so that total revenue increases.

3. Effective pricing objectives are designed to support corporate and marketing objectives and are flexible. Pricing objectives often focus on sales (to maximize sales or to increase market share), or they may specify a desired level of profit growth or profit margin. At other times, firms may develop pricing objectives for competitive effect, to increase customer satisfaction, or to communicate a certain image to prospective customers. Pricing objectives need to be flexible to adapt to different geographic areas and time periods.

A CASE ANALYSIS EXERCISE

1. Bojangles' was founded in Charlotte, North Carolina, in 1977, and specializes in Cajun Spiced Chicken and made-from-scratch buttermilk biscuits.

2. Randall Poindexter's job is to find the recipe for marketing success at Bojangles', a chain of fast food restaurants.

3. As Vice President of Marketing for the chain, his responsibilities include overseeing new store openings, developing individual market media plans and TV/radio creative advertising, and setting pricing strategies.

4. Currently the company that owns Bojangles' operates 224 restaurants (110 company-owned and 114 franchise-owned) in 7 states.

5. Bojangles' key strengths (which give them a competitive advantage) are their unique flavor profile, their fresh products, and their breakfast products served all day.

CHAPTER 13

PRICING METHODS

CHAPTER OVERVIEW

Effective pricing objectives are designed to support corporate and marketing objectives and are flexible. Like other elements in the marketing mix, pricing is influenced by a variety of external environmental factors including economic trends, the firm's competitive environment, changing cultural and demographic consumer trends, and the differences in the costs faced in different markets.

The most common types of pricing strategies are based on cost. Cost-based strategies include cost-plus pricing and price floor pricing. Pricing strategies which are based on demand require that marketers estimate the elasticity of demand in order to be assured they can sell what they produce. Specific strategies include demand backward pricing and chain-markup pricing. Strategies based on the competition may represent industry wisdom but can be tricky due to the responses of competitive firms. Examples of competition-based strategies include price leader strategy, parity pricing strategy, and limit pricing. Firms that focus on customer needs in developing pricing strategies may consider every-day-low-price or value pricing strategies, negotiated pricing policies, two-part pricing, or payment pricing. For multiple products, marketers may use price bundling or captive product pricing.

Pricing for members of the channel may include quantity discounts to encourage larger purchases, cash discounts to encourage fast payment, and seasonal discounts to spread purchases throughout the year or to increase in-season sales. Finally, geographic pricing tactics address differences in how far products must be shipped.

CHAPTER OBJECTIVES

1. Understand key pricing strategies.

2. Explain pricing tactics for individual and multiple products.

3. Describe the important psychological aspects of pricing.

4. Understand some of the legal and ethical considerations in pricing.

CHAPTER OUTLINE

Please refer to your textbook in order to define, list, and/or describe the missing parts of the chapter outline. The page numbers given will help guide you through this learning process.

I.   PRICE PLANNING: MOVE AND COUNTERMOVE _____
_____ *(p.349)*

II.   PRICING STRATEGIES _____ *(p.350)*
      A.   Pricing Strategies Based on Cost _____
            _____ *(p.350)*
            1.   Cost-Plus Pricing _____ *(p.351)*
            2.   Price-Floor Pricing _____ *(p.352)*
      B.   Pricing Strategies Based on Demand _____
            _____ *(p.353)*
            1.   Demand-Backward Pricing _____ *(p.353)*
            2.   Chain-Markup Pricing _____ *(p.354)*
      C.   Pricing Strategies Based on the Competition ____
            Price Leader _____ *(p.354)*
      D.   Pricing Strategies Based on Customers' Needs ___
            Value Pricing, or Everyday Low Pricing (EDLP) ___
            _____ *(p.355)*
      E.   New-Product Pricing
            1.   Skimming Price _____ *(p.356)*
            2.   Penetration Pricing _____ *(p.357)*
            3.   Trial Pricing _____ *(p.359)*

III. DEVELOPING PRICING TACTICS
      A.   Pricing For Individual Products
            1.   Two-Part Pricing _____ *(p.360)*
            2.   Payment Pricing _____ *(p.360)*
      B.   Pricing For Multiple Products
            1.   Price Bundling _____ *(p.360)*
            2.   Captive Pricing _____ *(p.361)*
      C.   Geographic Pricing
            1.   F.O.B. Pricing
                  F.O.B. Origin Pricing _____ *(p.361)*
                  F.O.B. Delivered Pricing _____ *(p.361)*
            2.   Zone Pricing _____ *(p.361)*
            3.   Uniform Delivered Pricing _____ *(p.362)*
            4.   Freight Absorption Pricing _____ *(p.362)*
      D.   Discounting For Members of The Channel
            1.   Trade or Functional Discounts
                  List Price _____ *(p.362)*
                  Trade or Functional Discounts ___ *(p.362)*
            2.   Quantity Discounts _____ *(p.363)*
                  Cumulative Quantity Discounts ___ *(p.363)*
                  Noncumulative Quantity Discounts ___
                  _____ *(p.363)*
            3.   Cash Discounts _____ *(p.363)*
            4.   Seasonal Discounts _____ *(p.363)*

  D. Pricing With Electronic Commerce _____
                      _____ *(p.364)*

IV. PSYCHOLOGICAL ISSUES IN PRICING
  A. Buyers' Pricing Expectations
    1. Internal Reference Prices _____
                    _____ *(p.364)*
    2. Price-Quality Inferences _____
                    _____ *(p.365)*
  B. Psychological Pricing Strategies
    1. Odd-Even Pricing _____ *(p.366)*
    2. Price Lining _____ *(p.366)*

V. LEGAL AND ETHICAL CONSIDERATIONS IN PRICING
  A. Deceptive Pricing Practices
    Bait-and-Switch _____ *(p.368)*
  B. Unfair Sales Acts
    Loss Leader Pricing _____ *(p.368)*
    Unfair Sales Acts _____ *(p.368)*
  C. Price Discrimination _____ *(p.368)*
  D. Price Fixing _____ *(p.368)*
  E. Horizontal Price Fixing _____ *(p.369)*
    1. Vertical Price Fixing _____ *(p.369)*

KEY TERMS

Select the correct term for each definition and write it in the space provided.

Price bundling
Chain-markup pricing
Price-floor pricing
Cumulative quantity discounts
Quantity discounts
Skimming price
Captive pricing
Zone pricing

Parity pricing
Trial pricing
Price leader
List price
Demand-based pricing
Penetration pricing
Cost-plus pricing

1. _____   A very high, premium price that a firm charges for its new, highly desirable product. *(p.356)*

2. _____   Pricing a new product low for a limited period of time in order to lower the risk for a customer. *(p.359)*

3. _____   A method of setting prices in which the seller adds up all the costs for the product and then adds an amount for overhead and profit. *(p.351)*

4. _____ A method for calculating price in which a portion of a firm's output may be sold at a price which only covers marginal costs of production in order to maintain full plant operating capacity. *(p.352)*

5. _____ A method of setting prices which is based on an estimate of demand at different prices. *(p.353)*

6. _____ A pricing strategy that extends demand-backward pricing from the ultimate consumer all the way back through channel of distribution to the manufacturer. *(p.354)*

7. _____ The firm that sets price first in an industry; other major firms in the industry follow the leader by setting similar prices. *(p.354)*

8. _____ A pricing tactic in which customers in different geographic zones pay different transportation rates. *(p.361)*

9. _____ A pricing strategy in which a firm sets a price low enough to match the competition, but still high enough to make a profit. *(p.354)*

10. _____ Discounts based on the total quantity bought within a specified time period. *(p.363)*

11. _____ A pricing strategy in which a new product is introduced at a very low price in order to encourage more customers to purchase the new product. *(p.357)*

12. _____ Selling two or more goods or services as a single package for one price. *(p.360)*

13. _____ A pricing tactic for two items that must be used together; one item is priced very low and the firm makes its profit on another high-margin item essential to the operation of the first item. *(p.361)*

14. _____ The price the end-customer is expected to pay as determined by the manufacturer. *(p.362)*

15. _____ A pricing strategy of charging reduced prices for purchases of larger quantities of a product by members of the channel of distribution. *(p.363)*

MULTIPLE CHOICE
Identify the most correct answer.

1. Pricing strategies based on the competition: *(p.354)*
   a. usually focus on a target level of profit growth.
   b. mean the pricing plan is specifically directed at having a certain effect on the marketing efforts of the competition.
   c. offer the lowest prices available so as to increase market share.
   d. emphasize that profits result from making customers satisfied.

2. Generally, firms that do business in an oligopoly are likely to: *(p.354)*
   a. adopt status quo pricing objectives in which pricing is linked to the competition.
   b. focus on nonprice competition.
   c. price each product based on its cost without much concern for matching the exact price of the competitors' products.
   d. focus on more value for the same price as the competition.

3. If the prices (and other characteristics) of two products are fairly close, it is likely that the consumer will feel the product quality is similar. This is called: *(p.365)*
   a. a price/quality relationship.
   b. the contrast effect.
   c. an assimilation effect.
   d. all of the above.

4. The most common form of cost-plus pricing is straight mark-up pricing, which: *(p.352)*
   a. is based on the costs involved in producing the product.
   b. occurs when price is calculated by adding a set percentage to the cost.
   c. calculates price by looking at both costs and what can be done to assure that a plant can operate at its capacity.
   d. subtracts a percentage of the cost from the cost to determine the selling price.

5. A method for setting prices which starts with a customer-pleasing price; the firm uses creative cost-management strategies in order to produce the product at a cost which will allow the firm to sell the product at that price is called: *(p.353)*
   a. price-floor pricing.
   b. demand pricing.
   c. chain-markup pricing.
   d. demand-backward pricing.

6. The parity pricing structure sets prices relative to an important industry reference point is known as: *(p.354)*
   a. competitor pricing.
   b. limit pricing.
   c. point pricing.
   d. reference pricing.

7. A pricing strategy in which a firm sets prices which provide ultimate value or price/benefit ratio to customers is: *(p.355)*
   a. limit pricing.
   b. value pricing or every day low pricing (EDLP).
   c. negotiated pricing.
   d. reference pricing.

8. A strategy in which a firm charges a very high premium price for its new, highly desirable product is: *(p.356)*
   a. dumping.
   b. penetration pricing.
   c. skimming price.
   d. pioneering price.

9. Pricing a new product low for a limited period of time in order to lower the risk for a customer is called: *(p.359)*
   a. limit pricing.
   b. penetration pricing.
   c. acceptance pricing.
   d. trial pricing.

10. An advertiser purchasing space in a group of magazines at a total package price is an example of: *(p.360)*
    a. captive pricing.
    b. price banding.
    c. price bundling.
    d. group pricing.

11. Seasonal discounts are: *(p.363)*
    a. price reductions offered only during certain times of the year.
    b. enticements to customers to pay their bills by the end of the season.
    c. options for customers to put seasonal items on lay-away.
    d. strategies to make customers accept shipment of a product by the end of the season.

12. The practice of charging different amounts for products depending on how far they must be shipped is: *(p.361)*
    a. regional pricing.
    b. geographic pricing.
    c. distance pricing.
    d. delivery pricing.

13. F.O.B. factory means that: *(p.361)*
    a. the supplier will pay to have the product loaded onto a truck or some other carrier.
    b. both the cost of loading and transporting to the customer is included in the selling price and will be paid by the manufacturer.
    c. the cost of transportation is the responsibility of the factory.
    d. the cost of transporting the product from the factory to the customer's location is the responsibility of the customer.

14. Uniform delivered pricing means: *(p.362)*
    a. that distant customers pay more while customers who are close to the factory pay less for the product.
    b. the seller absorbs the total cost of transportation.
    c. adding an average shipping cost to price.
    d. none of the above.

15. When the seller absorbs the total cost of transportation, this is known as: *(p.362)*
    a. freight absorption pricing.
    b. zone pricing.
    c. base-location pricing.
    d. designated pricing.

CHAPTER IN REVIEW - WRITING TO LEARN

1. Discuss pricing objectives typically used in planning pricing strategies.

_____

_____

_____

2. Explain pricing tactics for individual and multiple products.

_____

_____

_____

3. Describe the pricing strategies discussed that are based upon the competition.

_____

_____

_____

A Case Analysis Exercise

Real People, Real Choices: Meet Craig Lambert, A Decision Maker at Courtyard by Marriott

Reread the Opening Vignette on page 349 of your text and answer the following questions.

1. What position does Craig Lambert presently hold at Courtyard by Marriott?

2. How long has he been employed by Marriott?

3. In which division of Marriott did Mr. Lambert spend his first ten years of service with the company?

4. What is the primary responsibility of Craig Lambert with Courtyard by Marriott?

5. What group did Mr. Lambert join in 1983?

ANSWERS
CHAPTER OUTLINE

I. PRICE PLANNING: MOVE AND COUNTERMOVE--How companies develop and manage pricing strategies, and some of the specific tactics that put pricing strategies in action.

II. PRICING STRATEGIES--Can be based on costs, demand, the competition, and customer needs – as well as strategies for new products.
   A. Pricing Strategies Based on Cost--Marketers use cost-

based strategies because they are simple to calculate and relatively safe.
1. Cost-Plus Pricing--Method of setting prices in which the seller totals all the costs for the product and then adds the desired profit per unit.
2. Price-Floor Pricing--A method for calculating price in which, to maintain full plant operating capacity, a portion of a firm's output may be sold at a price that only covers marginal costs of production.

B. Pricing Strategies Based on Demand--A price-setting method based on estimates of demand at different prices.
1. Demand-Backward Pricing--Starts with a customer-pleasing price followed up with cost-management strategies to hold costs to a satisfactory level.
2. Chain-Markup Pricing--A pricing strategy that extends demand-backward pricing from the ultimate consumer all the way back through the channel of distribution to the manufacturer.

C. Pricing Strategies Based on the Competition
Price Leader--The firm that sets price first in an industry; other major firms in an industry follow the leader by staying in line.

D. Pricing Strategies Based on Customers' Needs
Value Pricing, or Every Day Low Pricing (EDLP)--A pricing strategy in which a firm sets prices which provide ultimate value to customers.

E. New Product Pricing
1. Skimming Price--A very high, premium price that a firm charges for its new, highly desirable product.
2. Penetration Pricing--A pricing strategy in which a new product is introduced at a very low price to encourage more customers to purchase it.
3. Trial Pricing--Pricing a new product low for a limited period of time in order to lower the risk for a customer.

III. DEVELOPING PRICING TACTICS
A. Pricing For Individual Products
1. Two Part Pricing--Two separate types of payments are required to purchase the product.
2. Payment Pricing--Breaking up the total price into smaller amounts payable over time.

B. Pricing for Multiple Products
Price Bundling--Selling two or more goods or services as a single package for one price.
Captive Pricing--A pricing tactic for two items that must be used together; one item is priced very low and the firm makes its profit on another, high-margin item essential to the operation of the first item.

C. Geographic Pricing
    1. F.O.B. Pricing
        F.O.B. Origin Pricing--A pricing tactic in which
        the cost of transporting the product from the
        factory to the customer's location is the
        responsibility of the customer.
        F.O.B. Delivered Pricing--A pricing tactic in which
        the cost of loading and transporting to the
        customer is included in the selling price and will
        be paid by the manufacturer.
    2. Zone Pricing--A pricing tactic in which customers
        in different geographic zones pay different
        transportation rates.
    3. Uniform Delivered Pricing--A pricing tactic in
        which a standard shipping charge is added to the
        price for all customers regardless of the distance
        from the seller.
    4. Freight Absorption Pricing--A pricing tactic in
        which the seller absorbs the total cost of
        transportation.
D. Discounting For Members of the Channel
    1. Trade or Functional Discounts
        List Price--The price the end customer is expected
        to pay as determined by the manufacturer.
        Trade or Functional Discounts--Discounts off list
        price of products to members of the channel of
        distribution that perform various marketing
        functions.
    2. Quantity Discounts--A pricing tactic of charging
        reduced prices for purchases of larger quantities
        of a product.
        Cumulative Quantity Discounts--Discounts based on
        the quantity bought within a specified time period.
        Noncumulative Quantity Discounts--Discounts based
        only on the quantity purchased with individual
        orders.
    3. Cash Discounts--Incentives offered by firms to try
        to entice their customers to pay their bills
        quickly.
    4. Seasonal Discounts--Price reductions offered only
        during certain times of the year.
E. Pricing With Electronic Commerce--Technology is creating
    a pricing revolution.

IV. PSYCHOLOGICAL ISSUES IN PRICING
    A. Buyers' Pricing Expectations
        1. Internal Reference Prices--A set or a price range
            in consumers' minds that they refer to in
            evaluating a product's price.
        2. Price-Quality Inferences--When consumers use price
            as a cue or an indicator for quality.
    B. Psychological Pricing Strategies

170

1. Odd-Even Pricing--Marketers have assumed that there is a psychological response to odd prices that differs from the responses to even prices.
2. Price Lining--The practice of setting a limited number of different specific prices, called price points, for items in a product line.

V. LEGAL AND ETHICAL CONSIDERATIONS IN PRICING
   A. Deceptive Pricing Practices
      Bait-And-Switch--An illegal marketing practice in which an advertised price special is used as bait to get customers into the store with the intention of switching them to a higher-priced item.
   B. Unfair Sales Act
      Loss Leader Pricing--The pricing policy of setting prices below cost in order to attract customers into a store.
      Unfair Sales Acts--State laws that prohibit suppliers from selling products below cost to protect small businesses from larger competitors.
   C. Price Discrimination--The Robinson-Patman Act includes regulations against price discrimination - the illegal practice of offering the same product to different business customers at different prices and thus lessening competition.
   D. Price Fixing--The collaboration of two or more firms in setting prices, usually to keep prices high.
   E. Horizontal Price Fixing--When competitors making the same product jointly determine what price they will charge.
      1. Vertical Price Fixing--When manufacturers or wholesalers attempt to force retailers to charge a certain price for their product.

ANSWERS

KEY TERMS

1. Skimming price
2. Trial pricing
3. Cost-plus pricing
4. Price-floor pricing
5. Demand-based pricing
6. Chain-markup pricing
7. Price leader
8. Zone pricing
9. Parity pricing
10. Cumulative quantity discounts
11. Penetration pricing
12. Price bundling
13. Captive pricing

MULTIPLE CHOICE

1. b
2. a
3. c
4. b
5. d
6. a
7. b
8. c
9. d
10. c
11. a
12. b
13. d

14. List price	14. c
15. Quantity discounts	15. a

CHAPTER IN REVIEW - WRITING TO LEARN

1. Effective pricing objectives are designed to support corporate and marketing objectives and are flexible. Pricing objectives often focus on sales (e.g., to maximize sales or to increase market share) or may specify a desired level of profit growth or profit margin. At other times, firms may develop pricing strategies designed to pre-empt the competition or to increase customer satisfaction.

2. To implement pricing strategies with individual products, marketers may use two-part pricing or payment pricing tactics. For multiple products, marketers may use price bundling, wherein two or more products are sold and priced as a single package. Captive pricing is often chosen when two items must be used together; one item is sold at a very low price and the other at a high, profitable price.

3. Strategies based on the competition may represent industry wisdom but can be tricky due to the responses of competitive firms. A price leader strategy is often used in an oligopoly where it is best for all to avoid competition. A parity pricing strategy means that a firm sets the same price as competitors. Limit pricing occurs when a firm sets a low price for a new product in order to discourage new competitors.

A CASE ANALYSIS EXERCISE

1. Mr. Craig Lambert is senior vice president and brand manager of Courtyard by Marriott.

2. Mr. Lambert has spent over 25 years with the company.

3. Mr. Lambert spent the first 10 years of his career in Marriott's Hotel division as a group sales manager.

4. Mr. Lambert is responsible for business planning, product design, and brand positioning efforts around the world.

5. In 1983, he joined a new Marriott lodging group to introduce Courtyard.

CHAPTER 14

CHANNEL MANAGEMENT, WHOLESALING, AND PHYSICAL DISTRIBUTION: DELIVERING THE PRODUCT

CHAPTER OVERVIEW

The main purpose of this chapter is to explain what a distribution channel is and describe its functions in the marketing mix. A distribution channel is an organized network of firms that work together to get a product from a producer to a customer. Channels provide time, place and ownership utility for customers.

Manufacturer-owned channel members include sales branches, sales offices, and manufacturers' showrooms. Merchant wholesalers and merchandise agents and brokers are examples of independent intermediaries. Consumer distribution channels include direct distribution where the producer sells directly to consumers and indirect channels which may include a wholesaler and/or a retailer. Business-to-business channels are often direct but may include industrial distributors, jobbers or dealers.

We next discussed the different types of decisions which must be made in distribution planning. Distribution planning begins with developing objectives which often relate to the amount of market penetration. Next, marketers must consider environmental factors such as the characteristics of the product, existing channel relationships, intermediary availability, the number and density of customers, customer needs, and the distribution channels of competitors before they select the type of channel and the number of channel members. Vertical marketing systems are channels in which there is cooperation at the different levels. Horizontal marketing systems are composed of firms at one channel level who work together.

Lastly, we explored the types of decisions made in physical distribution planning. Physical distribution involves moving goods from the manufacturer to the customer in, hopefully, the most efficient and effective manner possible. Physical distribution includes sorting and grading of goods, order processing, materials handling, warehousing, transportation, and inventory control.

CHAPTER OBJECTIVES

1. Explain what a distribution channel is and what functions distribution channels perform.

2. Describe some of the types of wholesaling intermediaries found in distribution channels.

3. Discuss the steps in planning distribution channel strategies.

4. Describe the activities that are important in the physical distribution of goods.

CHAPTER OUTLINE
Please refer to your textbook in order to define, list, and/or describe the missing parts of the chapter outline. The page numbers given will help guide you through this learning process.

I. PLACE: THE FINAL FRONTIER _____
   _____ *(p.380)*

II. THE IMPORTANCE OF DISTRIBUTION: YOU CAN'T SELL
    WHAT ISN'T THERE!
    A. What is a Distribution Channel? _____
       _____ *(p.381)*
       Channel Intermediaries _____
       _____ *(p.381)*
    B. Functions of Distribution Channels _____
       _____ *(p.381)*
       Breaking Bulk _____ *(p.382)*
       Creating Assortments _____ *(p.382)*
       Facilitating Functions _____ *(p.382)*

III. THE COMPOSITION AND STRUCTURE OF CHANNELS
     A. Types of Wholesaling Intermediaries _____
        _____ *(p.383)*
        1. Independent Intermediaries _____ *(p.383)*
           Merchant Wholesalers _____ *(p.383)*
           a. Full-Service Merchant Wholesaler ___
              _____ *(p.384)*
              Rack Jobber _____ *(p.384)*
           b. Limited-Service Merchant Wholesaler __
              _____ *(p.384)*
              Cash-and-Carry Wholesalers ___ *(p.384)*
              Truck Jobbers _____ *(p.385)*
              Drop Shippers _____ *(p.385)*
              Mail-Order Wholesalers _____
              _____ *(p.385)*
           Merchant Agents or Brokers _____ *(p.385)*
              Manufacturers' Agents _____ *(p.385)*
              Selling Agents _____ *(p.385)*
              Commission Merchants _____ *(p.386)*
              Merchandise Brokers _____ *(p.386)*
        2. Manufacturer-Owned Intermediaries _____
           _____ *(p.386)*
           Sales Branches _____ *(p.386)*
           Sales Offices _____ *(p.386)*
           Manufacturers' Showrooms _____ *(p.386)*

B.   Types of Distribution Channels _____ (p.386)
         Channel Levels _____ (p.386)
         1.   Consumer Channels _____ (p.386)
             Manufacturer-Retailer-Consumer Channel
             Manufacturer-Wholesaler-Retailer-Consumer Channel
         2.   Business-to-Business Channels _____ (p.389)
         3.   Distribution Channels for Services _____ (p.389)
         4.   Dual Distribution Systems _____ (p.389)

IV. PLANNING A CHANNEL STRATEGY _____ (p.390)
     A.   Channel Objectives _____ (p.390)
     B.   Evaluating the Environment _____ (p.392)
     C.   Choosing a Distribution System _____ (p.392)
         1.   Conventional, Vertical, and Horizontal Systems
             Conventional Marketing System _____ (p.392)
             Vertical Marketing System _____ (p.392)
             Horizontal Marketing System _____ (p.393)
         2.   Intensive, Exclusive, and Selective Distribution
             Intensive Distribution _____ (p.395)
             Exclusive Distribution _____ (p.395)
             Selective Distribution _____ (p.395)
     D.   Developing Distribution Tactics _____ (p.396)
         1.   Selecting Channel Partners _____ (p.396)
         2.   Managing the Channel of Distribution
             Channel Leader _____ (p.396)
     D.   Distribution Channels and the Marketing Mix _____ (p.397)

V.   PHYSICAL DISTRIBUTION
     A.   What is Physical Distribution? _____ (p.398)
         1.   Order Processing _____ (p.398)
         2.   Warehousing _____ (p.398)
         3.   Materials Handling _____ (p.399)
         4.   Transportation _____ (p.399)
         5.   Inventory Control _____ (p.401)

KEY TERMS
Select the correct term for each definition and write it in the space provided.

Direct channel
Horizontal marketing system
Channel levels
Warehousing
Merchant wholesaler
Vertical marketing system (VMS)
Creating assortments
Exclusive distribution

Merchandise handling
Channel of distribution
Intensive distribution
Conventional marketing
    system
Breaking bulk
Indirect distribution
Channel leader

1. _Channel of distrib._   An organized network of firms that work together to get a product from a producer to a consumer or business customer. *(p.381)*

2. _Merchant wholesaler_   Intermediaries who buy goods from producers (i.e., take title to them) and sell to other producers, wholesalers, and retailers. *(p.383)*

3. _Channel level_   The number of distinct intermediaries who populate a channel of distribution. *(p.386)*

4. _Direct channel_   A channel of distribution in which there are no intermediaries or middle levels. *(p.381)*

5. _Indirect_   Distribution of goods in which manufacturers reach end-users through intermediaries--wholesalers, dealers, distributors, agents and/or retailers. *(p.381)*

6. _Creating assortment_   Providing a variety of products in one location to meet the needs of buyers. *(p.382)*

7. _Conventional MKG syst_   A multiple-level distribution channel in which channel members work independently to perform channel functions. *(p.392)*

8. _Vertical MKG system_   A channel of distribution in which there is cooperation among members of the manufacturing, wholesaling, and retailing levels. *(p.392)*

9. _Merchandise handling_   The moving of products into, within, and out of warehouses. *(p.399)*

10. _Horizontal Mktg system_   An arrangement within a channel of distribution in which two or more firms at one channel level work together for a common purpose. *(p.394)*

11. _Intensive distribution_   Selling a product through all suitable wholesalers or retailers who are willing to stock and sell the product. *(p.395)*

12. _Exclusive distribution_   Selling a product only through a single outlet in a particular region. *(p.395)*

13. _Channel leader_   A firm at one level of distribution which takes a leadership role, establishing operating norms and processes that reduce channel conflicts, reduce costs, and enhance delivered customer value. *(p.396)*

14. _Warehouse_   Storing goods in anticipation of sale or transfer to another member of the channel of distribution. *(p.398)*

15. _Breaking bulk_   Dividing larger quantities of goods into smaller lots in order to meet the needs of buyers. *(p.382)*

MULTIPLE CHOICE
Identify the most correct answer.

1. Effective channels of distribution provide the following physical distribution function(s): *(p.382)*
   a. Breaking bulk.
   b. Creating assortments.
   c. Reducing transactions.
   d. All of the above.

2. Sales branches are: *(p.386)*
   a. wholesaler-type facilities owned and run by a manufacturer.
   b. typically located in strategic geographic areas in order to be closer to customers and there are no inventories.
   c. producer-owned facilities where customers visit to examine the firm's products attractively displayed.
   d. set up by manufacturers only in order to reduce selling costs.

177

3. Full-function wholesalers who regularly call on retailers are: (p.384)
   a. general-merchandise wholesalers.
   b. limited-line wholesalers.
   c. rack jobbers.
   d. drop shippers.

4. Manufacturers' agents: (p.385)
   a. handle the entire product line of one or more producers.
   b. are independent salespeople who carry the product lines of noncompeting manufacturers.
   c. assist in the sale of products by identifying likely buyers and sellers, bringing them together, and helping them make a purchase agreement.
   d. typically are found in agricultural markets such as grain, livestock, and produce.

5. Export/import intermediaries that facilitate transactions in markets such as real estate, food, and used equipment are known as: (p.386)
   a. commission merchants.
   b. sales agents.
   c. merchandise brokers.
   d. sales brokers.

6. Reason(s) why some manufacturers decide to sell directly to their customers rather than delegating this task to channel intermediaries include: (p.388)
   a. There are some instances where the direct channel allows the customer to be better served at a lower cost.
   b. When the producer handles distribution, it maintains control of pricing, service, delivery--all of the elements of the transaction.
   c. Direct distribution is sometimes the only way to gain customer interest in a new product.
   d. All of the above.

7. Business-to-business distribution channels are: (p.389)
   a. networks designed to facilitate the flow of goods from a producer to an organizational or business customer.
   b. the most common form of distribution channels in consumer markets.
   c. frequently used when products are distributed through very large retailers.
   d. more frequently indirect channels than in consumer markets.

8. If the product is being distributed through more than one type of channel, this is called: *(p.389)*
   a. vertical distribution.
   b. disorganized distribution.
   c. dual or multiple distribution.
   d. horizontal distribution.

9. Not only do marketers need to consider who is buying and why they are buying but they must know: *(p.392)*
   a. the distance from the producer to the manufacturer.
   b. the demographics of customers in the market.
   c. the functions that a distributor must perform to meet customer needs.
   d. all of the above.

10. In an administered VMS: *(p.392)*
    a. cooperation among members at the manufacturing, wholesaling, and retailing levels is legally enforced.
    b. voluntary cooperation is enforced by a channel leader.
    c. independent firms sign contracts that spell out how they will cooperate.
    d. retail members of a chain typically use a common name, cooperate in advertising and other promotions, and even develop their own private-label products.

11. Types of contractual VMSs include: *(p.393)*
    a. wholesaler-sponsored voluntary chains.
    b. retailer cooperatives.
    c. franchises.
    d. all of the above.

12. Distribution using fewer outlets than in intensive distribution but more than in exclusive distribution is: *(p.396)*
    a. selective distribution.
    b. independent distribution.
    c. conventional distribution.
    d. midpoint distribution.

13. The ability of the carrier to deliver goods, safely and on time is: *(p.399)*
    a. speed of delivery.
    b. dependability.
    c. capability.
    d. accessibility.

14. A process developed to insure that there is always available the types and quantities of goods needed to meet customers' demands is: *(p.401)*
    a. materials handling.
    b. order processing.
    c. inventory control.
    d. trade loading.

15. A system of distribution that reduces storing and handling costs with smaller and more frequent orders, thus matching supply and use is: *(p.403)*
    a. first-in first-out (FIFO).
    b. quick-response replenishment system.
    c. last-in first-out (LIFO).
    d. electronic data interchange (EDI).

CHAPTER IN REVIEW - WRITING TO LEARN

1. Explain what a distribution channel is and describe its functions in the marketing mix.

_____

_____

_____

2. Describe the characteristics of vertical marketing systems (VMSs).

_____

_____

_____

3. Identify the primary activities that are involved in physical distribution.

_____

_____

_____

A Case Analysis Exercise

Real People, Real Choices: Meet Cecelia Gardner, A Decision Maker at First Union National Bank

Reread the Opening Vignette on page 380 of your text and answer the following questions.

1. Who is Cecelia Gardner?

2. How did Cecelia Gardner begin her career in banking?

3. Describe the size of First Union National Bank.

4. Describe the competitive challenges facing First Union.

5. What positions had Cecelia Gardner held before being advanced to her current position as project manager?

ANSWERS
CHAPTER OUTLINE

I.   PLACE: THE FINAL FRONTIER--Making goods and services available where and when customers need and want them.

II. THE IMPORTANCE OF DISTRIBUTION: YOU CAN'T SELL WHAT ISN'T THERE!
     A. What is a Distribution Channel?--A series of firms or individuals that facilitates the movement of a product from a producer to the final customer.
         Channel Intermediaries---Firms or individuals such as wholesalers, agents, brokers, or retailers who help move a product from the producer to the consumer or business user.
     B. Functions of Distribution Channels--Channels provide time, place, and ownership utility for customers. In addition, channels increase the efficiency of the flow of goods from producer to consumer.
         Breaking Bulk--Dividing larger quantities of goods into smaller lots in order to meet the needs of buyers.
         Creating Assortments--Providing a variety of products in one location to meet the needs of buyers.
         Facilitating Functions---Functions of channel intermediaries that make the purchase process easier for customers and manufacturers.

III. THE COMPOSITION AND STRUCTURE OF CHANNELS
   A.   Types of Wholesaling Intermediaries--Firms that handle the flow of products from the manufacturer to the retailer or business user.
      1.   Independent Intermediaries--Channel intermediaries that are not controlled by any manufacturer but instead to business with many different manufacturers and many different customers.
         Merchant Wholesalers--Intermediaries that buy goods from manufacturers (take title to them) and sell to retailers and other business-to-business customers.
         a.   Full-Service Merchant Wholesaler---Provide a wide range of services for their customers (delivery, credit, etc.).
            Rack Jobber--Supplies retailers with specialty items.
         b.   Limited-Service Merchant Wholesaler--Provide fewer services for their customers.
            Cash-and-carry wholesalers--Provide low-cost merchandise for retailers and industrial customers who are too small for other wholesalers' sales representatives to call on them.
            Truck Jobbers--Carry their products to small business customer locations for their inspection and selection.
            Drop shippers--Limited function wholesalers that take title to the merchandise but never actually take possession of it.
            Mail-order wholesalers--Sell products to small retailers and other industrial customers, through catalogs.
         Merchant Agents or Brokers--Channel intermediaries that provide services in exchange for commissions but never take title to the product.
         Manufacturers' Agents--(Manufacturers' reps), are independent salespeople who carry several lines of noncompeting products.
         Selling Agents--(Including export/import agents) market a whole product line or one manufacturer's total output.
         Commission Merchants--Sales agents who receive goods, on consignment, while taking possession of the products without taking title.
         Merchandise Brokers--Identify likely buyers and sellers and bring the two together in return for a fee received.
      2.   Manufacturer-Owned Intermediaries--Separate business units that perform all of the functions of independent intermediaries, while maintaining complete control over the channel.

Sales Branches--Manufacturer-owned facilities that carry inventory and provide sales and service to customers in a specific geographic area.
Sales Offices--Like agents, they do not carry inventory but provide selling functions for the manufacturer in a specific geographic area.
Manufacturers' Showrooms--Facilities in which products are permanently displayed for customers to visit.

   B.   Types of Distribution Channels--Marketing manager must select a channel structure that creates a competitive advantage for the firm and its products based on the size and needs of the target market.
Channel Levels--The number of distinct intermediaries who populate the channel of distribution.

       1.   Consumer Channels--The simplest channel is a direct channel, (the manufacturer sells directly to customers).
Manufacturer-Retailer-Consumer Channel.
Manufacturer-Wholesaler-Retailer-Consumer Channel.

       2.   Business-to-Business Channels--Direct channels are more common here than in consumer markets.

       3.   Distribution Channels For Services--Most services travel directly from the producer to the consumer.

       4.   Dual Distribution Systems--When manufacturers, dealers, wholesalers, retailers, and customers interact with more than one type of channel.

IV.   PLANNING A CHANNEL STRATEGY--A focus on the distribution planning of producers or manufacturers because of the leadership role accepted in creating a successful distribution channel.

   A.   Channel Objectives--Develop appropriate objectives that support the organization's overall marketing goals.

   B.   Evaluating the Environment--Marketers must consider their internal and external environments.

   C.   Choosing a Distribution System--Three basic decisions include: the number of levels in the distribution channel, channel relationships, and the distribution intensity.

       1.   Conventional, Vertical, and Horizontal Systems
Conventional Marketing System--A multiple-level distribution channel in which channel members work independently of one another.
Vertical Marketing System--A channel of distribution in which there is cooperation among members at the manufacturing, wholesaling, and retailing levels.
Horizontal Marketing System--An arrangement within a channel of distribution in which two or more firms at the same channel level work together for a common purpose.

2. Intensive, Exclusive, and Selective Distribution
   Intensive Distribution--Selling a product through all suitable wholesalers or retailers that are willing to stock and sell the product.
   Exclusive Distribution--Selling a product only through a single outlet in a particular region.
   Selective Distribution--Distribution using fewer outlets than in intensive distribution but more than in exclusive distribution.

D. Developing Distribution Tactics--Decisions concerning the type of distribution system to use such as a direct or indirect channel, or a conventional or an integrated channel.
   1. Selecting Channel Partners--The channel relationship may be affected by the contribution level of each member concerning profit, service, and control.
   2. Managing the Channel of Distribution
      Channel Leader--A firm at one level of distribution that takes a leadership role, establishing operating norms and processes that reduce channel conflicts, reduce costs, and enhance delivered customer value.

E. Distribution Channels and the Marketing Mix--Place decisions affect pricing.

V. PHYSICAL DISTRIBUTION
   A. What is Physical Distribution?--The activities used to move finished goods from manufacturers to final customers including order processing, warehousing, materials handling, transportation, and inventory control.
      1. Order Processing--The activities that occur between the time an order is received and shipped.
      2. Warehousing--Storing goods in anticipation of sale or transfer to another member of the channel of distribution.
      3. Materials Handling--The moving of products into, within, and out of warehouses.
      4. Transportation--The modes of transportation include railroads, pipelines, water transportation, motor carriers, and airways, each differing in dependability, cost, speed of delivery, accessibility, capability and traceability.
      5. Inventory Control--Activities to ensure that goods are always available to meet customers' demands.

ANSWERS

KEY TERMS

1. Channel of distribution
2. Merchant wholesalers
3. Channel levels
4. Direct channel
5. Indirect distribution
6. Creating assortments
7. Conventional marketing system
8. Vertical marketing system (VMS)
9. Merchandize handling
10. Horizontal marketing system
11. Intensive distribution
12. Exclusive distribution
13. Channel leader
14. Warehousing
15. Breaking bulk

MULTIPLE CHOICE

1. d
2. a
3. c
4. b
5. c
6. d
7. a
8. c
9. c
10. b
11. d
12. a
13. b
14. c
15. b

CHAPTER IN REVIEW - WRITING TO LEARN

1. A distribution channel is an organized network of firms that work together to get a product from a producer to a customer. Channels provide time, place and ownership utility for customers. Channel members handle the physical distribution function for products including the breaking and accumulation of bulk, creating assortments, reducing the number of transactions necessary for the flow of goods, transportation and storage. Intermediaries in channels of distribution also perform a variety of both communications and facilitating functions.

2. Vertical marketing systems (VMSs) are channels in which there is cooperation at the different levels. VMSs include administered and contractual VMSs, wholesaler sponsored voluntary chains, retailer cooperatives, franchises and corporate VMSs.

3. Physical distribution involves moving goods from the manufacturer to the customer in, hopefully, the most efficient and effective manner possible. Physical distribution includes sorting and grading of goods, order processing, materials handling, warehousing, transportation, and inventory control.

A CASE ANALYSIS EXERCISE

1. Cecelia Gardner is Senior Vice President and Project Manager for Consumer Reengineering at First Union National Bank.

2. Cecelia Gardner began her career in banking as a clerk with First Union in 1978, after receiving a B.A. in psychology from the University of South Carolina.

3. First Union is the sixth largest bank in the United States with $235 billion in assets and 2,500 branches.

4. Gardner knows that competition in the banking industry and changes in electronic commerce are making it imperative for banks to be where consumers want them in the next century.

5. Before occupying her current position as project manager for consumer reengineering, she was a branch manager, consumer credit sales manager, and general banking group executive.

CHAPTER 15

RETAILING AND DIRECT MARKETING: BUYING THE PRODUCT

CHAPTER OVERVIEW

We began this chapter by explaining the position of retailing in the marketplace. Any person or organization that offers something for sale to a consumer is a retailer. The wheel of retailing hypothesis suggests that new retailers compete on price and then move upscale leaving room for other new low-price entrants. The retail life cycle theory suggests retailing institutions are introduced, grow, reach maturity, and then decline.

We learned about some of the environmental changes which will have an impact on the future of retailing as represented in demographic changes, technological developments, environmentally conscious consumers, and market globalization.

Retailers are classified by NAICS codes based on the product lines sold or according to whether they carry items which have high or low gross margins and/or high or low turnover rates. Types of retailers classified by the merchandise assortment carried are convenience stores, supermarkets, specialty stores, discount stores, department stores, mass merchandisers, and hypermarkets. In developing a retailing strategy, marketers seek to develop a desirable store image which includes atmospherics, store personnel, pricing policy, and store location.

Nonstore retailing includes traditional mail-order shopping, direct selling operations, and vending machines as well as newer forms of direct marketing such as television shopping, telemarketing, and on-line shopping. Finally, we learned about the opportunities and barriers to electronic commerce.

CHAPTER OBJECTIVES

1. Explain how retailing has evolved and how it continues to change.

2. Describe how retailers may be classified by type or selection of merchandise.

3. Understand the importance of store image to a retail positioning strategy and explain some of the actions a retailer can take to create a desired image in the marketplace.

4. Describe the major forms of nonstore retailing.

5. Describe the opportunities and barriers to electronic commerce in retailing.

CHAPTER OUTLINE
Please refer to your textbook in order to define, list, and/or describe the missing parts of the chapter outline. The page numbers given will help guide you through this learning process.

I.   RETAILING: SPECIAL DELIVERY _____ (p.409)
     A.   Retailing: A Mixed (Shopping) Bag) _____
          _____ (p.410)
     B.   The Evolution of Retailing
          1.   The Wheel of Retailing (Hypothesis)_____
               _____ (p.410)
          2.   The Retail Life-Cycle _____
               _____ (p.410)
     C.   The Evolution Continues: What's "In Store"
          For the Future _____ (p.411)
          1.   Demographics _____ (p.411)
          2.   Technology _____
               _____ (p.412)
          3.   Globalization _____ (p.413)

II. TYPES OF RETAILERS
     A.   Classifying Retailers by What They Sell _____
          _____ (p.414)
          1.   Product Lines: What is Sold _____ (p.414)
          2.   Product Type: Profit and Frequency _____ (p.414)
     B.   Classifying Retailers by the Selection of
          Merchandise They Sell
          Merchandise Assortment_____ (p.415)
          Merchandise Breadth_____ (p.415)
          Merchandise Depth_____ (p.415)
          1.   Convenience Stores_____ (p.416)
          2.   Supermarkets_____ (p.416)
          3.   Specialty Stores_____ (p.416)
          4.   Discount Stores_____ (p.416)
               Off-Price Retailers_____ (p.416)
               Mass Merchandisers_____ (p.416)
          5.   Department Stores_____ (p.417)
          6.   Hypermarkets_____ (p.417)

III. DEVELOPING A STORE POSITIONING STRATEGY:
     RETAILING AS THEATER_____ (p.417)
     A.   Store Image_____ (p.418)
          Atmospherics_____ (p.419)
          1.   Store Design: Setting the Stage _____ (p.419)
          2.   The Actors: Store Personnel_____ (p.422)
          3.   Pricing Policy: How Much for a Ticket
               to the Show?_____ (p.422)

B.   Building the Theater: Store Location
Types of Store Locations_____
_____ (p.423)
1.   Site Selection: Choosing Where to Build _____
_____ (p.424)

IV.   NONSTORE RETAILING
Nonstore Retailing_____ (p.427)
Direct Marketing_____ (p.427)
A.   Mail Order_____ (p.427)
1.   Catalogs_____ (p.427)
2.   Direct Mail_____ (p.428)

B.   Direct Selling_____ (p.428)
1.   Door-to-Door Sales_____ (p.428)
2.   Parties and Networks _____ (p.428)
3.   Telemarketing_____ (p.429)
C.   Automatic Vending_____ (p.429)
D.   Direct-Response Television _____ (p.429)
1.   Infomercials _____ (p.430)
2.   Home Shopping Networks _____ (p.430)
E.   Electronic Commerce: Back to the Future _____ (p.430)
1.   The Allure of Electronic Commerce _____ (p.430)
2.   Barriers to Success _____ (p.431)
3.   On-Line Shopping: Surfers' Paradise or a Drop
In the Bucket _____ (p.432)

KEY TERMS

Select the correct term for each definition and write it in the space provided.

Hypermarkets
Merchandise breadth
Multilevel network
Wheel of retailing hypothesis
Specialty stores
Point of Sale (POS) systems
Inventory turnover
Non store retailing

Retail life cycle theory
Direct marketing
Traffic flow
Supermarkets
Department stores
Merchandise depth
Store image

1. _____   A theory that explains how retail firms change, becoming more "upscale" as they go through their life cycle. *(p.410)*

2. _____   A process that focuses on the various life cycles stages from introduction to decline. *(p.410)*

189

3. _____ The direction in which shoppers will move through the store and what areas they will pass or avoid. *(p.419)*

4. _____ The average number of times a year a retailer expects to sell its inventory. *(p.415)*

5. _____ The number of different product lines available. *(p.415)*

6. _____ The variety of choices available for each specific product. *(p.415)*

7. _____ Food stores that carry a wide selection of edibles and related products. *(p.416)*

8. _____ Retailers who carry only a few product lines but offer good selection within the lines they do sell. *(p.416)*

9. _____ Retailers who sell a broad range of items and a good selection within each product line sold. *(p.417)*

10. _____ Retailers with the characteristics of both warehouse stores and supermarkets; hypermarkets are several times larger than other stores and offer virtually everything from grocery items to electronics. *(p.417)*

11. _____ The way a retailer is perceived in the marketplace relative to the competition. *(p.418)*

12. _____ Any method used to complete an exchange with a product end-user that does not require a customer visit to a store. *(p.427)*

13. _____ Exposing a consumer to information about a good or service through a nonpersonal medium and convincing the customer to respond with an order. *(p.427)*

14. _____ A system in which a master distributor recruits other people to become distributors, sells the company's product to the recruits, and receives a commission on all the merchandise sold by the people recruited. *(p.528)*

15. _____ Retail computer systems that collect sales data and are hooked directly into the store's inventory control system. *(p.412)*

MULTIPLE CHOICE
Identify the most correct answer.

1. In the introduction stage of the retail life cycle theory: *(p.410)*
   a. the concept of the business catches on and profits go up.
   b. market share stabilizes and profits decline.
   c. the new retailer often is an aggressive entrepreneur who takes a unique approach to doing business.
   d. the retail business becomes obsolete.

2. The range of products sold is known as: *(p.415)*
   a. merchandise assortment.
   b. merchandise breadth.
   c. merchandise depth.
   d. merchandise width.

3. Neighborhood retailers that carry a limited number of frequently purchased items including basic food products, newspapers, and sundries and cater to consumers who are willing to pay a premium for the ease of buying close to home are: *(p.416)*
   a. supermarkets.
   b. convenience stores.
   c. specialty stores.
   d. discount stores.

4. Retailers who offer a wide variety of inexpensive brand name items at low prices with minimal service are: *(p.416)*
   a. off-price retailers.
   b. factory outlet stores.
   c. hypermarkets.
   d. general merchandise discount stores.

5. Mass merchandisers: *(p.417)*
   a. offer a broad assortment of items.
   b. do not feature the depth of assortment found in department stores.
   c. emphasize well-known brand names at low prices.
   d. all of the above.

6. The way a retailer is perceived in the marketplace relative to the competition is called: (p.418)
   a. store image.
   b. retailer acceptability.
   c. store design.
   d. retailer effectiveness.

7. The use of color, lighting, scents, furniture, and other design elements to create a desired store image is: (p.419)
   a. store design.
   b. store layout.
   c. atmospherics.
   d. store definition.

8. The basic types of retail locations include: (p.423)
   a. business districts.
   b. shopping centers.
   c. freestanding retailers.
   d. all of the above.

9. A Central Business District (CBD): (p.423)
   a. refers to a smaller area with at least one department or variety store at a major intersection.
   b. is a shopping area where public transportation is usually available.
   c. evolves to satisfy convenience-oriented neighborhood shopping needs.
   d. features a greater diversity of merchandise.

10. A store's trading area is affected by: (p.426)
    a. its proximity to a population center.
    b. the number of anchor stores in the shopping district.
    c. the sharing of costs.
    d. the pricing of the merchandise.

11. The U.S. Census of Retailing divides nonstore retailing into the following category or categories: (p.427)
    a. mail order.
    b. indirect-selling establishments.
    c. automatic retailing machine operators.
    d. all of the above.

12. When a company representative makes a sales presentation to a group of people who have gathered in the home of a friend or acquaintance, this is known as: (p.428)
    a. a home shopping club.
    b. telemarketing.
    c. a home shopping party.
    d. direct mail.

13. Door-to-door selling is declining markedly in the U.S. due to: *(p.428)*
    a. women feeling richer at the office.
    b. the large numbers of houses that are empty during the day due to the increase in working women.
    c. the increasing reluctance of those who are at home to admit strangers.
    d. all of the above.

14. Hyperspace is: *(p.431)*
    a. a program by the software companies to increase the number of electronic retailing web sites.
    b. allowing the user to move from link to link at his or her own discretion.
    c. the newest marketing campaign of a major Internet company to switch customers to their service.
    d. a computer virus that has invaded certain electronic catalogs.

15. Example(s) of barriers to success of electronic commerce include: *(p.431)*
    a. Shoppers receive instant gratification from electronic commerce.
    b. Customers readily provide sensitive data such as credit card numbers.
    c. People need "touch and feel" information before buying many products.
    d. all of the above.

CHAPTER IN REVIEW - WRITING TO LEARN

1. Describe how retailers may be classified by type or selection of merchandise.

   _____

   _____

   _____

2. Identify and describe the major types of retail locations.

   _____

   _____

   _____

3. Explain what is considered "Nonstore Retailing".

_____

_____

_____

A Case Analysis Exercise

Real People, Real Choices: Meet Göran Carstedt, A Decision Maker at IKEA

Reread the Opening Vignette on page 409 of your text and answer the following questions.

1. Where is IKEA based and from where does the majority of its sales originate?

2. Who founded IKEA, and how was the name chosen?

3. What is IKEA's mission statement?

4. When did Göran Carstedt join IKEA?

5. What job has Göran Carstedt held at IKEA since 1995?

ANSWERS
CHAPTER OUTLINE

I. RETAILING: SPECIAL DELIVERY---Retailing is the final stop in the distribution channel by which goods and services are sold to consumers for their personal use.
    A. Retailing: A Mixed (Shopping) Bag--Part of what makes retailing such an exciting area is that the same good or service can be obtained in so many different ways.
    B. The Evolution of Retailing
        1. The Wheel of Retailing (Hypothesis)--A theory that explains how retail firms change, becoming more "upscale" as they go through their life cycle.
        2. The Retail Life Cycle--A process that focuses on the various life cycle stages from introduction to decline.
    C. The Evolution Continues: What's "In Store" For the Future--Three important factors motivate innovative merchants to reinvent the way they do business.

1. Demographics--Retailers need to constantly refine their merchandise mix to meet the needs of a changing market.
    a. Working Women--The dramatic increase in the number of working women has made the problem of "time poverty" even more acute.
    b. Age Segmentation--Retailers are increasingly recognizing that consumers in different age groups vary dramatically in terms of what they look for in a retail environment--and also have nurtured a healthy respect for the spending power of both young people and senior citizens.
    c. Ethnic Diversity--Although members of every ethnic group can usually find small, local retailers that understand and cater to their specific needs and subculture, larger operations must begin to tailor their strategies to the cultural makeup of specific trading areas.
2. Technology
    a. Technological Developments--Exciting new developments are constantly being introduced by retailers.
    Point of Sale (POS) Systems--Retail computer systems that collect sales data and are hooked directly into the store's inventory control system.
    b. Environmental Developments--Both traditional retailers and nonstore retailers also are taking steps to minimize the damage they do to the environment.
3. Globalization
    a. Globalization is a two-way street--Innovative European retailing concepts are influencing U.S. retailing.

II. TYPES OF RETAILERS
    A. Classifying Retailers by the Types of Merchandise They Sell--One of the most important strategic decisions a retailer has to make is what to sell--its merchandise.
        1. Product Lines: What is Sold--The Census of Retail Trade, conducted by the U.S. Bureau of the Census, classifies all retailers by SIC codes.
        2. Product Type: Gross Margin and Turnover--Another important distinction is how the characteristics of the particular products a store carries affect its ability to make a profit.
        Gross Margin--Revenue minus the cost of goods sold, calculated as a percentage of sales; the amount a retailer makes on an item.

Inventory Turnover--The average number of times a year a retailer expects to sell its inventory.

B. Classifying retailers by the Selection of Merchandise They Sell

Merchandise Assortment--The range of products sold.

Merchandise Breadth--The number of different product lines available.

Merchandise Depth--The variety of choices available for each specific product.

1. Convenience Stores--Neighborhood retailers that carry a limited number of frequently purchased items including basic food products, newspapers, and sundries and cater to consumers who are willing to pay a premium for the ease of buying close to home.

2. Supermarkets--Food stores that carry a wide selection of edibles and related products.

3. Specialty Stores--Retailers who carry only a few product lines but offer good selection within the lines they do sell.

4. Discount Stores--Retailers who offer a wide variety of inexpensive brand name items in a self-service, "no-frills" setting.

   Off-Price Retailers--Retailers who buy excess merchandise from well-known manufacturers and pass the savings on to customers.

   Mass Merchandisers--Retailers who offer a very large assortment of items.

5. Department Stores--Retailers who sell a broad range of items and a good selection within each product line sold.

6. Hypermarkets--Retailers with the characteristics of both warehouse stores and supermarkets; hypermarkets are several times larger than other stores and offer virtually everything from grocery items to electronics.

III. DEVELOPING A STORE POSITIONING STRATEGY: RETAILING AS THEATER--Many retailers recognize the importance of using visual and other sensory cues to create a store environment that reflects and perpetuates a desired image.

A. Store Image--The way a retailer is perceived in the marketplace relative to the competition.

   Atmospherics--The use of color, lighting, scents, furnishings, and other design elements to create a desired store image.

   1. Store Design--Some specific design decisions include store layout, fixture type and merchandise density, sound type and density, and color and lighting.

2. The Actors: Store Personnel--Store personnel should be carefully selected to complement a store's image.
3. Pricing Policy: How Much for a Ticket to the Show?--A store's pricing policy influences shoppers' perceptions of the "type" of store it is.

B. Building the Theater: Store Location
Types of Store Locations--There are four basic types of retail locations: A store can be found in a business district, in a shopping center, as a free standing entity, or in a nontraditional location.
1. Site Selection: Choosing Where to Build--Store location is a key strategic decision that affects economic aspects of a company's ability to operate effectively, turnover, and store image. Location planners often try to determine if an area needs a new store in the first place--put simply, locations can be evaluated in terms of whether they are saturated, understored, or overstored.

IV. NONSTORE RETAILING
Nonstore Retailing--Any method used to complete an exchange with a product end-user that does not require a customer visit to a store.
Direct marketing--Exposing a consumer to information about a good or service through a nonpersonal medium and convincing the customer to respond with an order.
A. Mail order--Today, consumers can buy just about anything through the mail.
1. Catalogs--Today, the catalog customer is more likely to be an affluent career woman who has access to more than enough stores, but who does not have the time or desire to go to them.
2. Direct Mail--A brochure or pamphlet offering a specific product or service at one point in time.

B. Direct Selling--Direct selling can be an effective approach, especially for products that require a great deal of information to sell.
1. Door-to-Door Sales--Door-to-Door selling is declining markedly in the U.S. due to the large numbers of homes that are empty during the day due to the increase in working women, the increasing reluctance of those who are at home to admit strangers, and women feeling richer at the office.
2. Parties and Networks--About three-quarters of direct sales are made in the consumer's home, sometimes at a home shopping party, at which a company representative makes a sales presentation to a group of people who have gathered in the home of a friend. In a multilevel network, a master distributor recruits other people to become distributors as well.

3. Telemarketing--The use of telemarketing, where prospective customers are contacted by phone, is a cheaper and easier method.
C. Automatic Vending--Coin-operated vending machines are a tried-and-true way to sell convenience goods, especially cigarettes and drinks.
D. Direct-Response Television--As early as 1950, television brought retailing into the viewer's living room.
1. Infomercials--Half-hour or hour commercials that resemble a talk show but are intended to sell something.
2. Home Shopping Networks--Television channels that exist solely to sell products.
E. Electronic Commerce: Back to the Future--Some of the most exciting developments in nonstore retailing can be found in the growing electronic marketplace--the use of computers to communicate product information and make transactions.
1. The Allure of Electronic Commerce--The ability to search for product information in hyperspace, in which the user can move from link to link at his or her discretion, is revolutionizing the shopping process for millions of intrepid surfers.
2. Barriers to Success--Barriers to electronic commerce include customer wait for products, no "touch and feel" information before buying, concern for security on the Internet, and concern of manufacturers angering store retailers.
3. On-Line Shopping: Surfers' Paradise or a Drop in the Bucket--We are just beginning to see the enormous potential of electronic commerce in retailing.

ANSWERS

KEY TERMS	MULTIPLE CHOICE
1. Wheel of retailing hypothesis	1. c
2. Retail life-cycle theory	2. a
3. Traffic flow	3. b
4. Inventory turnover	4. d
5. Merchandise breadth	5. d
6. Merchandise depth	6. a
7. Supermarkets	7. c
8. Specialty stores	8. d
9. Department stores	9. b
10. Hypermarkets	10. a
11. Store image	11. a
12. Nonstore retailing	12. c
13. Direct marketing	13. d
14. Multilevel network	14. b
15. Point of Sale (POS) system	15. c

CHAPTER IN REVIEW - WRITING TO LEARN

1. Retailers are classified by NAICS codes based on the product lines sold. Retailers may also be classified according to whether they carry items which have high or low gross margins and/or high or low turnover rates. Types of retailers classified by the merchandise assortment carried, that is, the assortment breadth and depth, are conveniences stores, supermarkets, specialty stores, discount stores, department stores, mass merchandisers, and hypermarkets.

2. Major types of retail locations include central business districts, secondary or neighborhood business districts, shopping centers, free-standing retailers, and new nontraditional locations. Retailers, in making store location decisions consider many different factors including the number of competing stores in an area, the proximity to population centers, the cost of locating a store in an area, and, of course, their ability to make a profit at the new location.

3. Nonstore retailing includes traditional mail-order shopping, direct selling operations, and vending machines as well as newer forms of direct marketing such as television shopping, telemarketing, and electronic retailing.

A CASE ANALYSIS EXERCISE

1. IKEA is based in Sweden but 70% of its sales come from beyond Scandinavia.

2. Ingvar Kamprad founded IKEA, and the name comes from his initials with the first letters of the Swedish farm, Elmtaryd and parish, Agunnaryd, where he grew up.

3. IKEA's mission statement is: "IKEA shall offer a wide range of home furnishing items of good design and function, at prices so low, that the majority of people can afford to buy them."

4. Göran Carstedt joined the IKEA organization in 1990, when he was named president of IKEA North America.

5. Since September 1995, Carstedt has been president of IKEA Europe and he is also overseeing the company's newly established corporate marketing staff.

CHAPTER 16

THE PROMOTION SUPERHIGHWAY

CHAPTER OVERVIEW

Marketers use a variety of communications tools to connect with customers. The four major elements of marketing communication are known as the promotion mix which include personal selling, advertising, sales promotions, and publicity and public relations. Marketers also communicate with customers through product and package design. Word-of-mouth communication from one consumer to another is often the most influential factor in consumer decisions.

Which promotion mix elements will be used depends on the overall strategy, i.e., a push versus a pull strategy, the type of product, the stage of the product life cycle, and the degree of buyer readiness and the type of buyer. Promotion budgets are often developed using rules of thumb and the specific strategies for the various mix elements are then planned and executed. Finally, marketers monitor and evaluate the promotion efforts to determine if objectives are being reached.

The traditional communications model includes a message source who creates an idea, encodes the idea into a message, and transmits the message through some medium. Today, marketers are focusing on interactive marketing where customized marketing communications elicit a measurable response from receivers. Database marketing is interactive marketing that utilizes a customized database and allows marketers to develop dialogues and build relationships with customers.

Integrated marketing communications (IMC) programs allow marketers to communicate with consumers on a continual basis by coordinating the promotion messages and media. In an IMC strategy, contact management means that communications occur when customers will be receptive to them. The effectiveness of the IMC strategy may be assessed through transactional data by customers' second-order responses, or by customer attitudes.

CHAPTER OBJECTIVES

1. Explain the goals of marketing communications.

2. List and describe the elements of the promotion mix.

3. Explain the steps in managing the promotion mix.

4. Compare the traditional model of communications with the current trend toward interactive promotion strategies.

5. Explain why database marketing is increasingly popular and how databases are developed and managed.

6. Explain integrated marketing communications, how an IMC program can be implemented, and why some marketers resist IMC.

CHAPTER OUTLINE
Please refer to your textbook in order to define, list, and/or describe the missing parts of the chapter outline. The page numbers given will help guide you through this learning process.

I. TAILORING MARKETING COMMUNICATIONS TO CUSTOMERS
    Promotion _____ (p.444)
    Promotion Goals _____ (p.445)

II. PROMOTIONAL STRATEGY
    A.   The Promotion Mix_____ (p.445)
        1.   Personal Appeals
            Personal Selling _____ (p.446)
        2.   Mass Appeals
            Advertising _____ (p.447)
            Sales Promotion _____ (p.447)
            Publicity and Public Relations ____ (p.447)
    B.   Managing The Promotion Mix
        Promotion Plan _____ (p.448)
        1.   Establish Promotion Objectives
            Create Awareness _____ (p.449)
            Inform the Market _____ (p.450)
            Create Desire _____ (p.450)
            Encourage Trial _____ (p.450)
            Build Loyalty _____ (p.450)
        2.   Identify Influences on the Promotion Mix
            Push Strategy _____ (p.450)
            Pull Strategy _____ (p.450)
            The Product Life Cycle Influencing The
            Promotion Mix _____ (p.451)
        3.   Determine and Allocate the Total Promotion
            Budget
            Top-Down Budgeting Techniques _____
            _____ (p.452)
            Percentage-of-Sales Method _____
            _____ (p.452)
            Competitive-Parity Method _____
            _____ (p.452)
            Bottom-Up Budgeting Techniques _____
            _____ (p.452)
            Objective-Task Method _____
            _____ (p.452)

    4.   Allocate the Budget to a Specific
         Promotion Mix
         Organizational Factors _____ *(p.453)*
         Market Potential _____ *(p.453)*
         Market Size _____ *(p.453)*
    5.   Evaluate the Effectiveness of the Promotion Mix
         _____ *(p.453)*

III. THE PROMOTION SUPERHIGHWAY: INTERACTIVE MARKETING
    A.   The Traditional Communications Model
         Communications Model _____ *(p.455)*
         1.   Encoding by the Marketer _____ *(p.455)*
         2.   The Source_____ *(p.456)*
         3.   The Message_____ *(p.456)*
         AIDA Model _____ *(p.456)*
         4.   The Medium_____ *(p.457)*
         5.   Decoding by the Receiver
         Receiver _____ *(p.457)*
         Decoding_____ *(p.457)*
         6.   Noise_____ *(p.457)*
         7.   Feedback_____ *(p.457)*
    B.   Redrawing the Traditional Communications Road
         Map: Interactive Marketing
         Interactive Marketing _____ *(p.458)*
         1.   Customizing the Message: De-Mass Marketing____
         _____ *(p.458)*
         2.   Levels of Interactive Response
         Transactional Data _____ *(p.458)*
    C.   The Bedrock of the Promotion Superhighway:
         Database Marketing
         Database Marketing _____ *(p.459)*

IV. PUTTING IT ALL TOGETHER AND HITTING THE OPEN ROAD:
    INTEGRATED MARKETING COMMUNICATIONS
    A.   Driving In Multiple Lanes:
         Coordinating Promotion Messages
         Integrated Marketing Communications (IMC)_____
         _____ *(p.460)*
         1.   Taking the Driver's Perspective_____ *(p.461)*
         2.   Highway Under Construction: The
             Emerging IMC Perspective_____ *(p.461)*
    B.   The IMC Planning Model: Begin with the Driver,
         Not the Engine
         1.   Start with a Customer Database
         2.   Develop Promotional Strategies
             Contact Management _____ *(p.462)*
         3.   Implementing Specific Promotional Tactics____
         _____ *(p.463)*
         4.   Evaluating IMC Communications_____ *(p.463)*
    C.   Roadblocks on the IMC Superhighway_____
         _____ *(p.463)*

CHAPTER 16

KEY TERMS
Select the correct term for each definition and write it in the space provided.

Promotion mix
Integrated marketing communications
    (IMC)
Decoding
Promotion plan
Source
Database marketing
Pull strategy
Noise

Push strategy
Message

Promotion
Communications model
Interactive marketing
Medium
Transactional data

1. _____   The coordination of efforts by a marketer to inform or persuade consumers or organizations about goods, services, or ideas. *(p.444)*

2. _____   The creation of an ongoing relationship with a set of customers who have an identifiable interest in a product and whose responses to promotional efforts become part of future communications attempts. *(p.459)*

3. _____   A strategy in which an organization coordinates the different types of communication, from advertising to company letterhead, to reach customers with a message that is clear, that is consistent, and that maintains this positive relationship with them over time. *(p.460)*

4. _____   The major elements of marketer-controlled communications including advertising, sales promotions, publicity and public relations, and personal selling. *(p.445)*

5. _____   An ongoing record of individuals or organizations that buy a product. *(p.458)*

6. _____   The elements necessary for meaning to be transferred from a sender to a receiver. *(p.455)*

7. _____ A document that outlines the strategies for developing, implementing and controlling the firm's promotion activities. *(p.448)*

8. _____ A promotion strategy in which a company tries to move its products through the channel by convincing channel members to offer them. *(p.450)*

9. _____ A promotion strategy in which a company tries to convince consumers to want their products in anticipation that retailers will stock the items demanded. *(p.450)*

10. _____ An organization or individual which send a message. *(p.456)*

11. _____ The communication in physical form is sent from a sender to a receiver. *(p.456)*

12. _____ A communications vehicle through which a message is transmitted to target audience. *(p.457)*

13. _____ The process of assigning meaning to the message by a receiver. *(p.457)*

14. _____ Anything that interferes with effective communication. *(p.457)*

15. _____ A promotion practice in which customized marketing communications elicit a measurable response from individual receivers. *(p.458)*

MULTIPLE CHOICE
Identify the most correct answer.

1. Promotion: *(p.444)*
   a. informs consumers about new goods and services, and where they can be obtained.
   b. reminds consumers to continue using familiar products.
   c. builds relationships with customers.
   d. all of the above.

2. Nonpersonal communication that is paid for by an identified sponsor using mass media to inform or persuade an audience is: *(p.447)*
    a. sales promotion.
    b. publicity.
    c. advertising.
    d. campaigning.

3. The big advantage of public relations is: *(p.447)*
    a. that when messages are successfully placed, they are more credible than if the same information appeared in a paid advertisement.
    b. that it is often used to create and reinforce a distinctive brand identity.
    c. the stimulation of immediate sales by providing extra value.
    d. that it gives retailers incentives to move a company's products out the door.

4. In order to create a desire for a product, a company may consider using: *(p.450)*
    a. an anonymous expert who advertises a product.
    b. a paid actor who participates in infomercial audiences.
    c. an expert or celebrity who has a vested interest in a product and advises others to use it.
    d. an expert who tries to minimize the effects of negative publicity.

5. When interest is heightened by not revealing the exact nature of the product, this is known as a(n): *(p.449)*
    a. teaser campaign.
    b. infomercial.
    c. private promotion.
    d. ghost advertisement.

6. Promotions must start to focus on communicating specific product benefits in the: *(p.451)*
    a. introduction phase.
    b. growth phase.
    c. maturity phase.
    d. decline phase.

7. The most commonly used top-down procedure in which the promotion budget is based on either last year's sales or on estimates of this year's sales is: *(p.452)*
    a. all-you-can-afford method.
    b. competitive-parity method.
    c. objective-task method.
    d. percentage-of-sales method.

8. Using this bottom-up approach, the firm first defines the specific communication goals it shapes to achieve and it then tries to figure to how much and what kind of promotion efforts it would take to meet that goal. *(p.452)*
   a. All-you-can-afford method.
   b. Competitive-parity method.
   c. Objective-task method.
   d. Percentage-of-sales method.

9. The process of translating an idea into a form of communication that will convey meaning is called: *(p.455)*
   a. descriptive analysis.
   b. decoding.
   c. semiotics.
   d. encoding.

10. An advertising strategy where a message contains both positive and negative information is called: *(p.457)*
    a. conclusive advertising.
    b. a two-sided message.
    c. representative advertising.
    d. a one-sided message.

11. The organization or individual which intercepts and interprets the message is known as the: *(p.457)*
    a. messenger.
    b. decoder.
    c. receiver.
    d. medium.

12. The reactions of the receiver to the message which are communicated back to the source are: *(p.457)*
    a. feedback.
    b. interactions.
    c. appeals.
    d. effectiveness.

13. A second-order response is: *(p.458)*
    a. a list of people who have an identifiable interest in the product.
    b. customer feedback in response to a promotional message that is not in the form of a transaction.
    c. a list of people who have a history of responding to direct marketing promotions.
    d. all of the above.

14. A list of individuals or organizations that have an identifiable interest in the product and a history of responding to direct marketing promotions is a: *(p.459)*
    a. response list.
    b. consumer interest list.
    c. compiled list.
    d. promotion list.

15. An ongoing record of individuals or organizations who are using your services or buying your product is called: *(p.458)*
    a. an overlayment.
    b. integrated data.
    c. a consumer track.
    d. transactional data.

CHAPTER IN REVIEW - WRITING TO LEARN
1. Explain the goals of marketing communications.

_____

_____

_____

2. List and describe the elements of the promotion mix.

_____

_____

_____

3. Describe database marketing and how marketers use it to satisfy customers.

_____

_____

_____

A Case Analysis Exercise

Real People, Real Choices: Meet Tom Eppes, President, Price/McNabb Focused Communications

Reread the Opening Vignette on page 444 of your text and answer the following questions.

1.   Why did Price McNabb spend three years restructuring?

2.   What is the key to integrated marketing?

3.   What is promotion?

4.   Describe how Price/McNabb operates differently from the more traditional advertising agency.

5.   What is database marketing?

ANSWERS
CHAPTER OUTLINE

I.   TAILORING MARKETING COMMUNICATIONS TO CUSTOMERS
     Promotion--The coordination of a marketers marketing communications efforts to influence attitudes or behavior.
     Promotion Goals---Promotion informs consumers about new goods and services, and where they can be obtained.   --Promotion reminds consumers to continue using products. --Promotion persuades consumers to chose one product over others.   -- Promotion builds relationships with customers.

II. PROMOTIONAL STRATEGY
     A.   The Promotion Mix--The major elements of marketer-controlled communications including advertising, sales promotions, publicity and public relations, and personal selling.
          1.   Personal Appeals
               Personal Selling--Direct interaction between a company representative and a customer, which can occur in person, by phone, or even over an interactive computer link.
          2.   Mass Appeals
               Advertising--Nonpersonal communication from an identified sponsor using mass media.
               Sales Promotion--Contests or store demonstrations designed to build interest in a specified product in a specified time.

Publicity and Public Relations--Seek a positive image for the product or company through press releases, staging events, and commissioning surveys.

B. Managing The Promotion Mix

Promotion Plan--A framework that outlines the strategies for developing, implementing, and controlling the firm's promotion activities.

1. Establish Promotion Objectives

Create Awareness--Make members of the target market aware that a new brand is available in the market.

Inform the Market--Provide prospective users with knowledge about the benefits the new product has to offer.

Create Desire--Create favorable feelings toward the product, and convince some to use the product.

Encourage Trial--The company now needs to get consumers who have expressed interest in the product to try it.

Build Loyalty--Convince customers to keep buying the product.

2. Identify Influences on Promotion Mix

Push Strategy--The company tries to move its products through the channel by convincing channel members to offer them.

Pull Strategy--The company tries to move its products through the channel by building desire for the products among consumers, thus convincing retailers to respond to this demand by stocking those items.

The Product Life Cycle Influencing the Promotion Mix--Introduction phase—build awareness. Growth phase—focus on specific benefits of product.

Maturity Phase—many people have tried product, sales promotions should increase. Decline phase—as sales fall so does a reduction in promotion spending.

3. Determine and Allocate the Total Promotion Budget

Top-Down Budgeting Techniques--Allocation of the promotion budget based on the total amount to be devoted to marketing communications.

Percentage-of-Sales Method--A method for promotion budgeting in which the promotion budget is based on a certain percentage of either last year's sales or on estimates for the present year's sales.

Competitive-Parity Method--Spending whatever competitors pay for promotion.

Bottom-Up Budgeting Techniques--Allocation of the promotion budget based on identifying promotional goals and allocating enough money to accomplish them.

Objective-Task Method--A promotion budgeting method in which an organization first defines the specific communication goals it hopes to achieve and then tries to calculate what kind of promotional efforts it will take to meet these goals.

4. Allocate the Budget to a Specific Promotion Mix
   Organizational Factors--Preferences within the company based on past experiences or specific goals.
   Market Potential--Allocate more resources in markets where consumers will be more likely to buy the product.
   Market Size--Larger markets are more expensive places in which to promote.

5. Evaluate the Effectiveness of the Promotion Mix
   Monitor and evaluate the company's promotional efforts.

III. THE PROMOTION SUPERHIGHWAY: INTERACTIVE MARKETING
   A. The Traditional Communications Model
      Communications Model--The elements necessary for meaning to be transferred from a sender to a receiver.

      1. Encoding by the Marketer--The process of translating an idea into a form of communication that will convey meaning.

      2. The Source--An organization or individual that sends a message.

      3. The Message--The communication in physical form which is sent from a sender to a receiver.
         AIDA Model--The communications goals of attention, interest, desire, and action.

      4. The Medium--A communications vehicle through which a message is transmitted to target audience.

      5. Decoding by the Receiver
         Receiver--The organization or individual that intercepts and interprets the message.
         Decoding--The process of assigning meaning to the message by a receiver.

      6. Noise--Anything that interferes with effective communication.

      7. Feedback--The reactions of the receiver to the message that are communicated back to the source.

   B. Redrawing the Communications Road Map: Interactive Marketing
      Interactive Marketing--A promotional practice in which customized marketing communications elicit a measurable response from individual receivers.

      1. Customizing the Message: De-Mass Marketing--Marketing to individuals rather than the masses.

      2. Levels of Interactive Response
         Transactional Data--An ongoing record of individuals or organizations that buy a product.

C. The Bedrock of the Promotion Superhighway: Database Marketing
Database Marketing--The creation of an ongoing relationship with a set of customers who have an identifiable interest in a product or service and whose responses to promotional efforts become part of future communications attempts.

IV. PUTTING IT ALL TOGETHER AND HITTING THE OPEN ROAD; INTEGRATED MARKETING COMMUNICATIONS
A. Driving in Multiple Lanes: Coordinating Promotion Messages
Integrated Marketing Communications (IMC)--A strategic business process used to plan, develop, create, and evaluate coordinated, measurable, persuasive brand communication programs over time with target audiences.
1. Taking the Driver's Perspective--The customer absorbs information about a product or organization from many sources.
2. Highway Under Construction: The Emerging IMC Perspective--Many advertising agencies, promotion companies, and manufacturers are beginning to develop their own ideas of what an IMC strategy should look like.
B. The IMC Planning Model: Begin with the Driver, Not the Engine
1. Start with a Customer Database
2. Develop Promotional Strategies
Contact Management--A communication strategy which seeks to provide communications exposures where and when the targeted customer is most likely to receive them.
3. Implementing Specific Promotional Tactics
The communications situation will then determine the type of message to be developed based upon the communications objectives and what response from recipients is required.
4. Evaluating IMC Communications--The dimensions that should be considered when measuring the effectiveness of an IMC campaign are first-order responses, second-order responses, and attitudes toward the brand and/or organization.
C. Roadblocks on the IMC Superhighway--Some of the barriers to the IMC approach that marketers are discovering include the approach requires changes in the way promotion strategies are planned and implemented; the approach assigns relatively more importance on aspects of promotion other than advertising; brand managers and

associate brand managers develop promotional strategies at lower levels after senior planners have already developed the larger marketing strategy; many advertising agencies feel that they should be the ones to provide "one-stop shopping" for promotion services.

CHAPTER 16
ANSWERS

KEY TERMS		MULTIPLE CHOICE
1.	Promotion	1. d
2.	Database marketing	2. c
3.	Integrated marketing communications (IMC)	3. a
4.	Promotion mix	4. c
5.	Transactional data	5. a
6.	Communications model	6. b
7.	Promotion plan	7. d
8.	Push strategy	8. c
9.	Pull strategy	9. d
10.	Source	10. b
11.	Message	11. c
12.	Medium	12. a
13.	Decoding	13. b
14.	Noise	14. a
15.	Interactive marketing	15. d

CHAPTER IN REVIEW - WRITING TO LEARN

1. Marketers use a variety of communications tools to connect with customers. Through promotion strategies marketers inform consumers about new products, remind them of familiar products, persuade them to choose one alternative over another, and build strong relationships with customers.

2. The four major elements of marketing communications are known as the promotion mix. Personal selling provides face-to-face contact between a company representative and customer. Advertising is nonpersonal communication from an identified sponsor using mass media. Sales promotions stimulate immediate sales by providing incentives to the trade or to consumers. Publicity and public relations activities seek to influence the attitude of various publics.

3. Database marketing is interactive marketing that utilizes a customized database. Database marketing allows marketers to develop dialogues and build relationships with customers. Marketers use database marketing to create programs that are more flexible, reward loyal users, locate new customers, offer related products to existing customers, i.e., cross-selling, and track customer responses.

A CASE ANALYSIS EXERCISE

1. Price/McNabb spent three years on restructuring to transform itself into a fully integrated marketing communications company.

2. The key to integrated marketing is to match products with people's preferences.

3. Promotion refers to the coordination of efforts by a marketer to inform or persuade consumers or organizations about goods, services, and ideals.

4. Unlike a traditional advertising agency, Price/McNabb develops communications programs for clients that combine the promotional elements of advertising, public relations, database marketing, and sales promotion.

5. Database marketing is the creation of an ongoing relationship with a set of customers who have an identifiable interest in a product and whose responses to promotion efforts become part of future communications attempts.

CHAPTER 17

ADVERTISING

CHAPTER OVERVIEW

The main purpose of this chapter is to explain advertising's role in marketing communications. Advertising is nonpersonal communication from an identified sponsor using mass media to persuade or influence an audience. The major types of advertising are consumer product advertising, trade advertising, and institutional advertising. Advertising begins with the client or advertiser who may be a manufacturer, a distributor, a retailer, or an institution. Advertising agencies create ads or other promotions and arrange for their delivery to the target market.

Planning of an advertising campaign begins with developing objectives. Next, advertisers develop a creative strategy which should create attention, interest, desire, and action. A media plan determines where and when advertising will appear. Broadcast media include television and radio. Print media refers to newspapers, magazines, and directories. In developing media schedules, planners consider the size and characteristics of each media vehicle's audience, the objectives of the media plan, the advertising of competitors, and the capabilities of the media.

While we can be confident that, in general, advertising does increase sales, advertisers need to conduct research to determine if specific advertisements are effective. Examples of types of research include pretesting or copy testing of advertising before placing it in the media and posttesting research.

Finally, there are important considerations in advertising to international markets. A standardized strategy may be used where the same ad campaign is used in different cultures and emphasizes similarities of consumers.

CHAPTER OBJECTIVES

1. Tell what advertising is and describe the major types of advertising.

2. Describe the major players in the advertising process.

3. Tell how advertisers develop an advertising campaign.

4. Describe the major advertising media and the important considerations in media planning.

5. Explain how advertisers evaluate the effectiveness of the campaign.

6. Discuss the challenges facing advertising.

CHAPTER OUTLINE
Please refer to your textbook in order to define, list, and/or describe the missing parts of the chapter outline. The page numbers given will help guide you through this learning process.

I. PROMOTIONAL MESSAGES: AND NOW A WORD FROM OUR SPONSOR. . .
   Advertising _____ (p.472)
   A. Types of Advertising
      1. Product Advertising_____ (p.474)
      2. Institutional Advertising_____ (p.474)
         Advocacy Advertising_____ (p.475)
         Public Service Advertisements _____
         _____ (p.475)
   B. Who Does Advertising? _____
      _____ (p.475)
      Advertising Campaign _____ (p.475)
      In-House Agency _____ (p.475)
      Limited Service Agency _____ (p.476)
      Full-Service Agency _____ (p.476)
      1. Many different tasks are required to produce
         a campaign
         Account Management _____
         _____ (p.476)
         Creative Services _____ (p.476)
         Research and Marketing Services _____
         _____ (p.476)
         Media Planning _____ (p.477)

II. DEVELOPING THE ADVERTISING CAMPAIGN
    A. Identify The Target Market _____ (p.477)
    B. Establish Message and Budget Objectives _____
       _____ (p.477)
       1. Setting Message Goals _____ (p.477)
       2. Setting the Budget _____ (p.478)
    C. Design The Ad
       Creative Strategy _____ (p.478)
       Advertising Appeal _____ (p.479)
       1. Common Advertising Appeals
          Reasons Why: The Unique Selling Proposition____
          _____ (p.479)
          Comparative Advertising _____ (p.479)
          Demonstration _____ (p.479)
          Testimonial _____ (p.480)
          Slice-of-Life _____ (p.480)
          Lifestyle _____ (p.480)
          RK Swamy/BBDO _____ (p.480)

          Fear Appeals _____ *(p. 481)*
          Sex Appeals _____ *(p. 481)*
          Humorous Appeals _____ *(p. 481)*
   D.   Pretest What Will Be Said
       Pretesting _____ *(p. 481)*
       Copy Testing _____ *(p. 481)*
       Copy Testing Techniques _____ *(p. 481)*
   E.   Choose The Media
       Media Planning _____ *(p. 481)*
       Aperture _____ *(p. 482)*
       1.   Types of Media: Where to Say It _____ *(p. 482)*
           Television _____ *(p. 482)*
           Radio _____ *(p. 482)*
           Newspapers _____ *(p. 484)*
           Magazines _____ *(p. 484)*
           Directories _____ *(p. 484)*
           Out-of-Home Media _____ *(p. 484)*
           Computer Media _____ *(p. 485)*
       2.   Media Scheduling: When to Say It
           Media Schedule _____ *(p. 485)*
           Advertising Exposure _____ *(p. 485)*
           Impressions _____ *(p. 485)*
           Reach _____ *(p. 486)*
           Frequency _____ *(p. 486)*
           Gross Rating Points _____ *(p. 486)*
           Cost Per Thousand _____ *(p. 487)*
       3.   Media Scheduling: How Often to Say It
           _____ *(p. 487)*

III. EVALUATING ADVERTISING
   A.   Pretesting _____ *(p. 488)*
       Unaided Recall _____ *(p. 488)*
       Aided Recall _____ *(p. 488)*
       Attitudinal Measures _____ *(p. 488)*
   B.   Challenges Facing the Advertising Industry _____
       _____ *(p. 489)*
   C.   How the Advertising Industry is Meeting the
       Challenges _____ *(p. 489)*

CHAPTER 17
KEY TERMS
Select the correct term for each definition and write it in the space provided.

Reach
Unique Selling Proposition (USP)
Advertising
Cost per thousand (CPM)
Creative strategy
Advertising appeal
Media schedule
Advocacy advertising

Media planning
Copy testing
Aided recall
Gross Rating Points (GRPs)
Product advertising
Frequency
Advertising campaign

1. _____ Nonpersonal communication paid for by an identified sponsor using mass media to persuade or inform. *(p.472)*

2. _____ An advertising message that focuses on a specific good or service. *(p.474)*

3. _____ A type of public-service advertising provided by an organization seeking to influence public opinion on an issue in which it has some stake in the outcome. *(p.475)*

4. _____ A coordinated, comprehensive communications plan that carries out promotion objectives and results in a series of advertisements placed in media over a period of time. *(p.475)*

5. _____ A research technique that uses clue to prompt answers from people about advertisements they might have seen. *(p.488)*

6. _____ The central idea or theme of an advertising campaign. *(p.479)*

7. _____ An advertising appeal which focuses on one clear reason why a particular product is superior. *(p.479)*

8. _____ The process that turns a concept into an advertisement. *(p.478)*

9. _____ The process of developing media objectives, strategies, and tactics for use in an advertising campaign. *(p.481)*

10. _____ The plan that specifies the exact media to use and when. *(p.486)*

11. _____ The percentage of the target market that will be exposed to the media vehicle. *(p.486)*

12. _____ The number of times a person in the target group will be exposed to the message. *(p.486)*

13. _____ A measure used for comparing the effectiveness of different media vehicles; average reach times frequency. *(p.486)*

14. _____ A measure used to compare the relative cost-effectiveness of different media vehicles that have different exposure rates; the cost to deliver a message to 1000 people or homes. *(p.487)*

15. _____ A marketing research method that seeks to measure the effectiveness of ads by determining whether consumers are receiving, comprehending and responding to the ad according to plan. *(p.481)*

MULTIPLE CHOICE
Identify the most correct answer.

1. In ancient Greece and Rome, advertisements of sorts appeared on: *(p.472)*
   a. walls and tablets.
   b. vases.
   c. tree trunks.
   d. togos.

2. Product advertising usually has the following purpose(s): *(p.474)*
   a. Educates people about a new product and what it does.
   b. Emphasizes a brand's features and tries to convince the target market to choose it over other options.
   c. Ensures that people won't forget about the product.
   d. All of the above.

3. On average, all U.S. businesses spend this much on advertising: *(p.472)*
   a. Ten percent of what they earn.
   b. Five percent of what they earn.
   c. Between 1 percent and 3 percent of what they earn.
   d. Between 15 percent and 20 percent of what they earn.

4. The most common form of advertising is: *(p.474)*
   a. business-to-business advertising.
   b. product advertising.
   c. institutional advertising.
   d. retail advertising.

5. Advocacy advertising is designed to: *(p.475)*
   a. create or enhance brand image.
   b. increase the distribution of products by persuading more retailers to carry them.
   c. influence public opinion on an issue of public service.
   d. none of the above.

6. Rather than focusing on a specific good or service, institutional advertising promotes: *(p.474)*
   a. the activities, "personality", or point of view of an organization.
   b. communication between manufacturers and businesses and organizations.
   c. an issue that is clearly in the public interest.
   d. the store's location, hours, price, and the availability of certain products.

7. An advertising campaign: *(p.475)*
   a. shares the cost of local advertising with a retailer.
   b. results in a series of advertisements placed in media over a period of time.
   c. evaluates the standing of different media vehicles in terms of their ability to deliver it to the desired consumer group.
   d. all of the above.

8. A disadvantage of television advertising is: *(p.483)*
   a. the reproduction quality of images is relatively poor.
   b. small audience of most stations means ads must be repeated frequently.
   c. hard to communicate complex messages.
   d. the audience is increasingly fragmented.

9. The account executive of an advertising agency: *(p.476)*
   a. is the person who actually dreams up and produces the ads.
   b. assists in designing and evaluating ad executions.
   c. is in charge of developing the campaign strategy for the client and ensuring that the advertising that is created will meet the client's desired objectives.
   d. all of the above.

10. To compare the relative cost-effectiveness of different media and of spots run on different vehicles in the same medium, media planners use a measure called: *(p.487)*
    a. cost per thousand (CPM).
    b. reach.
    c. effective demand.
    d. gross rating points (GRPs).

11. An aperture is: *(p.482)*
    a. the process that occurs when a concept is translated into an actual advertisement.
    b. the best place and time to reach a person in the target market group.
    c. the central idea of the message.
    d. the information to be presented about an item.

12. Comparative advertising is when: *(p.479)*
    a. the negative consequences of using or not using a product are highlighted.
    b. celebrity endorsers are used to differentiate a product from competitors.
    c. an emotional response in the receiver creates a desire for the product.
    d. two or more brands are compared by name.

13. The testimonial format of presenting information in an advertisement involves: *(p.480)*
    a. a speech where the source speaks directly to the audience in an attempt to inform them about a product or idea.
    b. the use of comparison, where the reader is told "A is B".
    c. a story about an abstract trait or concept that has been personified as a person, animal, vegetable, or mythical character.
    d. a celebrity, an expert, or a "typical person" stating how effective the product is.

14. Comparative advertisements: *(p.479)*
    a. are commercial messages arranged according to interest or topic.
    b. are inserts to the paper.
    c. explicitly names two or more competitors.
    d. consist of a product "in action" to prove it performs.

15. To calculate the exposure a message will have if placed in a certain medium, planners measure exposure by considering two factors: *(p.486)*
    a. reach and frequency.
    b. sales pattern and attention.
    c. quality and quantity.
    d. size and conveyance.

CHAPTER IN REVIEW - WRITING TO LEARN

1. Explain advertising's role in marketing goals.

_____

_____

_____

2. List and describe the major types of advertising.

_____

_____

_____

3. Explain some of the important considerations in media planning.

_____

_____

_____

A Case Analysis Exercise

Real People, Real Choices: Meet Anna Olofsson
A Decision Maker at A&O Analys

Reread the Opening Vignette on page 472 of your text and answer the following questions.

1. Who is Anna Olofsson?

2. What is A&O Analys?

3. Describe some of the businesses served by A&O Analys.

4. Discuss the research carried out by Anna Olofsson.

5. Describe the subject matter of the book Anna Olofsson has written.

ANSWERS
CHAPTER OUTLINE

I.   PROMOTIONAL MESSAGES: AND NOW A WORD FROM OUR SPONSOR. . .
     Advertising---Nonpersonal communication paid for by an
     identified sponsor using mass media to persuade or inform.
     A.   Types of Advertising
          1.   Product Advertising--An advertising message that
               focuses on a specific good or service.
          2.   Institutional Advertising--An advertising message
               that promotes the activities, personality, or point
               of view of an organization or company.
               Advocacy Advertising--A type of public service
               advertising provided by an organization that is
               seeking to influence public opinion on an issue
               because it has some stake in the outcome.
               Public Service Advertising--Advertising run by the
               media without charge for not-for-profit
               organizations or to champion a particular cause.
     B.   Who Does Advertising?--Creating and executing an
          advertising campaign often means many companies work
          together, and it requires a broad range of skilled
          people to do the job right.
          Advertising Campaign--A coordinated, comprehensive plan
          that carries out promotion objectives and results in a
          series of advertisements placed in media over a period
          of time.
          In-House Agency--Firms that do their own advertising.
          Limited-Service Agency--Provides one or more specialized
          service such as media buying or creative development.
          Full-Service Agency--Provides most or all of the
          services needed to mount a campaign, including research,
          creation of ad copy and art, media selection, and
          production of the final messages.
          1.   Many different tasks are required to produce a
               campaign.
               Account Management--The account executive or
               account manager develops the campaign's strategy
               for the client.
               Creative Services--Creatives are the "heart" of the
               communications effort.
               Research and Marketing Services--Researchers are
               the "brains" of the campaign.
               Media Planning--Recommends which communication
               vehicles are the most effective and efficient.

II. DEVELOPING THE ADVERTISING CAMPAIGN
     A.   Identify the Target Market--The target market is
          identified from research and segmentation decisions.
     B.   Establish Message and Budget Objectives--Advertising
          objectives should be consistent with the marketing plan.
          1.   Setting Message Goals--Message goals can be

increasing brand awareness, boosting sales by a certain percentage or even changing the image of a product.

    2.   Setting the Budget--The major approaches and techniques include the percentage-of-sales and objective-task methods.

C.   Design The Ad

Creative Strategy--The process that turns a concept into an advertisement.

Advertising Appeal--The central idea or theme of an advertising message.

    1.   Common Advertising Appeals

Reasons Why: The Unique Selling Proposition--An advertising appeal that focuses on one clear reason why a particular product is superior.

Comparative Advertising--Explicitly names two or more competitors.

Demonstration--The ad shows a product "in action" to prove that it performs as claimed.

Testimonial--A celebrity, an expert, or a "typical person" states the product's effectiveness.

Slice-of-Life--The format presents a (dramatized) scene from everyday life.

Lifestyle--This format shows a person or persons attractive to the target market in an appealing setting.

RK Swamy/BBDO--The goal, was to create ad messages that are warm and friendly.

Fear Appeals--The negative consequences of using or not using a product.

Sex Appeals--Some ads appear to be selling sex rather than products.

Humorous Appeals--Can be an effective way to break through advertising clutter.

D.   Pretest What Will Be Said

Pretesting--A research method that seeks to minimize mistakes by getting consumer reactions to ad messages before they are placed in the media.

Copy Testing--A marketing research method that seeks to measure the effectiveness of ads by determining whether consumers are receiving, comprehending, and responding to the ad according to plan.

Copy Testing Techniques--Concept Testing, Test Commercials, and Finished Testing.

E.   Choose the Media

Media Planning--The process of developing media objectives, strategies, and tactics for use in an advertising campaign.

Aperture--The best place and time to reach a person in the target market group.

1. Types of Media: Where to Say It--The major categories of media.
   Television--The ability to reach many people at once.
   Radio--Flexible, low cost, and the ability to reach specific consumer segments.
   Newspapers--An excellent medium for local advertising.
   Magazines--Flexibility and wide readership.
   Directories--The most "down-to-earth" information focused advertising.
   Out-of-Home Media--A communication medium that reaches people in public places.
   Computer Media--A communication medium that transmits information through the World Wide Web (WWW) or via e-mail messages.
2. Media Scheduling: When to Say It
   Media Schedule--The plan that specifies the exact media to be used and when.
   Advertising Exposure--The degree to which the target market will see an advertising message placed in a specific vehicle.
   Impressions---The number of people who will be exposed to a message placed in one or more media vehicles.
   Reach--The percentage of the target market that will be exposed to the media vehicle.
   Frequency--The number of times a person in the target group will be exposed to the message.
   Gross Rating Points--A measure used for comparing the effectiveness of different media vehicles; average reach times frequency.
   Cost Per Thousand--A measure used to compare the relative cost effectiveness of different media vehicles that have different exposure rates; the cost to deliver a message to 1,000 people or homes.
3. Media Scheduling: How Often To Say It--A continuous schedule, or pulsing schedule.

III. EVALUATING ADVERTISING
   A. Posttesting--Research conducted on consumers' responses to actual advertising messages they have seen or heard.
   Unaided Recall--A research technique conducted by telephone survey or personal interview that asks how much of an ad a person remembers during a specified period of time.
   Aided Recall--A research technique that uses clues to prompt answers from people about advertisements they might have seen.
   Attitudinal Measures--A research technique that probes a consumer's beliefs or feelings about a product before and after being exposed to messages about it.

B. Challenges Facing The Advertising Industry--An erosion of brand loyalty. Technology gives power back to the people. Greater emphasis on point-of-purchase factors. The rules are changing. The advertising environment is cluttered. Some consumers are turned off by advertising.

C. How the Advertising Industry is Meeting the Challenges—Establish a global reach, Diversity, Technology.

CHAPTER 17
ANSWERS

KEY TERMS

1. Advertising
2. Product advertising
3. Advocacy advertising
4. Advertising campaign
5. Aided recall
6. Advertising appeal
7. Unique Selling Proposition (USP)
8. Creative strategy
9. Media planning
10. Media schedule
11. Reach
12. Frequency
13. Gross Rating Points (GRPs)
14. Cost per thousand (CPM)
15. Copy testing

MULTIPLE CHOICE

1. a
2. d
3. c
4. b
5. c
6. a
7. b
8. d
9. c
10. a
11. b
12. d
13. d
14. c
15. a

CHAPTER IN REVIEW - WRITING TO LEARN

1. Advertising is nonpersonal communication from an identified sponsor using mass media to persuade or influence an audience. Advertising informs, reminds, and creates consumer desire. Advertising allows the organization to communicate its message in a favorable way and to repeat the message as often as it deems necessary for it to have impact on receivers.

2. Product advertising is used to persuade consumers to choose a specific product or brand. Institutional advertising is used to promote an entire organization (corporate image advertising), express the opinions of an organization (advocacy advertising), or to support a case (public service advertising).

3.	In developing media schedules, planners consider the size and characteristics of each media vehicle's audience, the objectives of the media plan (i.e., reach and frequency), the advertising of competitors, and the capabilities of the media. In comparing different media, planners examine the comparative cost efficiency of each media vehicle i.e., cost per thousand (CPM). Media planners must also decide when to deliver the messages or whether to use a continuous, pulsing, or flighting schedule.

A CASE ANALYSIS EXERCISE

1.	Anna Olofsson is account manager at A&O Analys.

2.	A&O Analys is a Swedish advertising agency focusing on strategic marketing consultation.

3.	A&O Analys works with food industry and high-tech companies with a special interest in the adolescent market.

4.	Anna Olofsson has done research on how popular culture influences the behaviors and product preferences of adolescents.

5.	Anna Olofsson has written a book on the consumption patterns of Generation X.

CHAPTER 18

SALES PROMOTION, PUBLIC RELATIONS AND PERSONAL SELLING

CHAPTER OVERVIEW

In this chapter, we first reviewed the purpose of public relations to maintain or improve the image of an organization among various publics. An important part of this is managing publicity. Public relations is important in introducing new products, influencing legislation, enhancing the image of a city, region or country, and calling attention to a firm's community involvement.

Next, we described the steps in developing a public relations campaign which begin with setting promotional objectives, examining the current attitudes of various publics, determining the issues of interest, and then planning what action to take. A PR campaign may include sponsorship of an event, cause-related marketing activities, and developing print or video news releases about timely topics.

Sales promotions are short-term programs designed to build interest in or encourage purchase of a product. Trade promotions include merchandise allowances, push money, trade shows, promotional products, and incentive programs.

Personal selling occurs when a company representative directly informs a client about a good or service to get a sale. Personal selling is more important for push strategies. Because of the high cost per customer contact, telemarketing is growing in popularity. Different types of salespeople include order takers, technical specialists, missionary salespeople, and order getters.

The steps in the personal selling process include prospecting, qualifying the prospects, the preapproach, the approach, making the sales presentation, overcoming customer objections, closing the sale, and follow up after the sale.

Finally, sales management means planning, implementing, and controlling the selling function. The responsibilities of a sales manager are setting sales force objectives and creating a sales force strategy, including specifying sales territories, recruiting, training, and rewarding salespeople.

CHAPTER OBJECTIVES

1. Explain the role of public relations and its function.

2. Describe the steps in developing a public relations campaign.

227

3. Explain what sales promotion is and describe some of the different types of trade and consumer sales promotion activities.

4. Explain the important role of personal selling in the marketing effort.

5. List the steps in the personal selling process.

6. Explain the job of the sales manager.

CHAPTER OUTLINE

Please refer to your textbook in order to define, list, and/or describe the missing parts of the chapter outline. The page numbers given will help guide you through this learning process.

I.   ADVERTISING'S NOT THE ONLY GAME IN TOWN! _____
     _____ *(P.497)*

II. PUBLIC RELATIONS_____ *(p.497)*
     Publicity _____ *(p.498)*
     A.   Objectives of Public Relations
          1.   _____ *(p.498)*
          2.   _____ *(p.499)*
          3.   _____ *(p.499)*
          4.   _____ *(p.499)*
          5.   _____ *(p.499)*
     B.   Planning a Public Relations Campaign
          1.   _____ *(p.499)*
          2.   _____ *(p.499)*
          3.   _____ *(p.500)*
               Press Release _____ *(p.500)*

III. SALES PROMOTION_____ *(p.502)*
     A.   Trade Promotion
          1.   Discounts and Deals _____ *(p.504)*
               Merchandise Allowance _____ *(p.504)*
               Case Allowance _____ *(p.504)*
          2.   Industry Boosting and Boasting
               Trade Shows _____ *(p.504)*
               Promotional Products _____ *(p.504)*
               Incentive Programs _____ *(p.504)*
               Push Money _____ *(p.504)*
     B.   Consumer Promotions
          1.   Price-Based Consumer Promotions _____
               _____ *(p.505)*
               Rebates _____ *(p.505)*
               Special Packs _____ *(p.505)*
          2.   Attention-Getting Consumer Promotions ____
               _____ *(p.505)*

Contests and Sweepstakes _____ (p.505)
Premiums _____ (p.506)
Sampling _____ (p.506)
Point-of-Purchase (POP) Promotion _____
_____ (p.506)
Cross-Promotion _____ (p.507)

IV. PERSONAL SELLING _____ (P.507)
    A.   The Role of Personal Selling
        Telemarketing _____ (p.508)
        Order Taker _____ (p.508)
        Technical Specialist _____ (p.508)
        Missionary Salesperson _____ (p.508)
        Order Getter _____ (p.508)
    B.   Approaches to Personal Selling _____
        _____ (p.509)
        1.   Transactional Marketing: Putting on the
            Hard Sell
            Transactional Selling _____ (p.509)
        2.   Relationship Selling: Countering the
            Tarnished Image
            Relationship Selling _____ (p.509)
    C.   The Role of Personal Selling in the
        Promotion Mix _____ (p.509)
    D.   The Selling Process _____ (p.509)
        Creative Selling Process _____ (p.509)
        1.   Prospect Customers
            Prospecting _____ (p.510)
        2.   Qualify Prospects _____ (p.510)
        3.   Do a Preapproach _____ (p.510)
        4.   Make the Approach _____ (p.511)
        5.   Make the Sales Presentation _____
            _____ (p.512)
        6.   Overcome Customer Objections _____
            _____ (p.512)
        7.   Close the Sale _____ (p.512)
        8.   Follow-Up After the Sale _____
            _____ (p.513)
    E.   Sales Management _____ (p.513)
        1.   Setting Sales Force Objectives _____
            _____ (p.513)
        2.   Creating a Sales Force Strategy _____
            _____ (p.513)
            Sales Territory _____ (p.513)
        3.   Recruiting, Training, and Rewarding Salespeople
            Recruiting _____ (p.514)
            Sales Training _____ (p.514)
            Rewarding Salespeople _____
            _____ (p.514)

CHAPTER 18

KEY TERMS
Select the correct term for each definition and write it in the space provided.

Rebate
Premiums
Publicity
Sales promotions
Telemarketing
Order getter
Order taker
Point-of-purchase (POP)

Coupons
Price deal
Qualify prospects
Public relations
Trade promotion objectives
Merchandise allowance
Press release

1. *Sales promotions*   Short-term programs to build interest in or encourage purchase of a product or service during a specified time period. *(p.502)*

2. *Merchand. allowance*   A type of trade sales promotion in which a manufacturer reduces prices to retailers. *(p.504)*

3. *Qualify prospects*   A part of the selling process that determines how likely prospects are to become customers. *(p.510)*

4. *Premiums*   Items that are offered to people who have purchased a product. *(p.506)*

5. *POP*   An element of sales promotion that includes displays and signs for use in the retail outlet. *(p.506)*

6. *Coupons*   Printed certificates redeemable for money off on a purchase. *(p.505)*

7. *Order getter*   A salesperson who works creatively to develop relationships with customers or to generate new sales. *(p.508)*

8. *Price deal*   A temporary price reduction offered by a manufacturer to stimulate sales. *(p.505)*

9. *Rebate*   A short-term offer that allows the consumer to get back part of the product's original cost by mail directly from the manufacturer. *(p.505)*

10. _Telemarketing_ : The use of the telephone to sell directly to consumers and business consumers. *(p.508)*

11. _Trade promotion objective_ : Among retailers, this goal is accomplished by encouraging decision makers to select the item, to stock it in larger quantities and/or to feature it prominently in retail advertising and on store shelves. *(p.503)*

12. _Order taker_ : A salesperson whose primary function is to facilitate transactions that are initiated by the customer. *(p.508)*

13. _Public relation_ : Activities or organizations aimed at influencing the way consumers, stockholders, and others feel about brands, companies, politicians, celebrities, non-profit organizations, or even governments. *(p.497)*

14. _Publicity_ : Unpaid communication in the mass media regarding a company, product, or event. *(p.498)*

15. _press release_ : A description of some event or news item that is sent to newspaper and magazine editors in the hope that it will be published as a news item. *(p.500)*

MULTIPLE CHOICE
Identify the most correct answer.

1. A person who contributes expertise in the form of product demonstrations, recommendations for complex equipment, set-up of machinery, or in-service education is a: *(p.508)*
   a. missionary salesperson.
   b. detailer.
   c. demo rep.
   d. technical specialist.

2. A promotion can be undertaken for many reasons, including the following: *(p.507)*
   a. Obtaining distribution or shelf space for a product.
   b. Decreasing the volume of product bought by a retailer.
   c. Creating lesser brand awareness among consumers.
   d. Discouraging consumers to try the product.

3. In general, promotions work best when: *(p.506)*
   a. they cement relationships with retailers and wholesalers.
   b. they present a tangible benefit to the consumer, such as giving something away or stressing attractive and innovative product displays.
   c. long-term changes in market share are created.
   d. firms practice database marketing.

4. A sales follow-up includes: *(p.513)*
   a. data on past sales, testimonial of other buyers, and guarantees.
   b. developing information about prospective customers.
   c. setting outcome goals.
   d. sales activities which provide important services to customers after the sale.

5. A case allowance provides: *(p.504)*
   a. a direct payment to the retailer for stocking a product.
   b. a discount to the retailer based on the volume of the product ordered.
   c. reimbursement to the retailer for in-store support.
   d. payment to a salesperson every time he or she sells an item.

6. Incentive programs are promotions that: *(p.504)*
   a. allow manufacturers to show off their product lines to wholesalers and retailers.
   b. employ useful or decorative items imprinted with an organization's identification, message, or logo.
   c. recognize superior achievements, as when salespeople meet or exceed specific sales objectives.
   d. involve the consumer in the company's marketing efforts.

7. A standard, memorized sales presentation is a: *(p.512)*
   a. canned sales presentation.
   b. selling-formula presentation.
   c. need-satisfaction presentation.
   d. hard-sell presentation.

8. The most popular form of sales promotion overall is: *(p.505)*
   a. free standing inserts (FSI's).
   b. in-store sampling.
   c. coupons.
   d. in-store displays.

9. The process of planning, implementing, and controlling the personal selling function of an organization is known as: *(p.513)*
   a. sales function.
   b. sales management.
   c. sales development.
   d. sales implementation.

10. Consumer promotion objectives are established to: *(p.506)*
    a. encourage decision-makers to select the item and stock it in larger quantities.
    b. build morale by demonstrating the level of support given to the product and by rewarding the salesforce for selling even more of it.
    c. feature an item prominently in retail advertising and on store shelves.
    d. stimulate impulse buying, reward loyal customers for continuing to buy the product, and to lure users of competing products away.

11. When two or more products or services combine forces to create interest using a single promotion tool, this is called: *(p.507)*
    a. cross-promotion.
    b. incentive-promotion.
    c. bonus-promotion.
    d. price deal.

12. The objective(s) of relationship selling include: *(p.509)*
    a. winning customers.
    b. keeping customers.
    c. developing customers.
    d. all of the above.

13. A high-pressure form of selling is: *(p.509)*
    a. the soft sell.
    b. the relationship approach.
    c. the hard sell.
    d. the hammer-over-the-head approach.

14. A public relations campaign plan should include the following element(s): *(p.499)*
    a. A statement of the problem.
    b. A marketing analysis.
    c. Discussion of how the program will be devaluated.
    d. All of the above.

15. A type of press release, features, includes: *(p.502)*
    a. topics in the news.
    b. articles about people associated with the organization who have done something of interest.
    c. reports on activities, services, and accomplishments of part of the entire organization.
    d. promotions of activities sponsored by the organization.

CHAPTER IN REVIEW - WRITING TO LEARN

1. Describe some of the advantages and disadvantages of sales promotions.

    _____

    _____

    _____

2. Describe some of the various types of trade promotions frequently used by marketers.

    _____

    _____

    _____

3. Describe the steps in developing a public relations campaign.

    _____

    _____

    _____

A Case Analysis Exercise

Real People, Real Choices: Meet Bunny Richardson, A Decision Maker at BMW Manufacturing

Reread the Opening Vignette on page 497 of your text and answer the following questions.

1. Describe what makes the BMW Manufacturing Corporation unique.

2. What is the present position held by Bunny Richardson at BMW?

3.   What is manufactured at the BMW Manufacturing Corporation?

4.   How did Bunny Richardson begin her career?

5.   Describe Bunny Richardson's first position at the BMW Manufacturing Corporation.

ANSWERS
CHAPTER OUTLINE

I.   ADVERTISING'S NOT THE ONLY GAME IN TOWN!--Three different promotional techniques can be used to make an impact, they include: public relations (free publicity), sales promotion (a focused campaign), and personal selling (delivering a sales pitch in person).

II. PUBLIC RELATIONS--Communications strategies to build good relationships with an organization's publics, including consumers, stockholders, and legislators.
Publicity--Unpaid communication about an organization appearing in the mass media.
   A.   Objectives of Public Relations
      1.   Introducing new products to manufacturers.
      2.   Introducing new products to consumers.
      3.   Influencing government legislation.
      4.   Enhancing the image of a city, region, or country.
      5.   Calling attention to a firm's involvement with the community.
   B.   Planning a Public Relations Campaign
      1.   The organization must first develop clear objectives for the PR program that define the message it wants people to hear.
      2.   The PR specialist then creates a campaign strategy that includes: a statement of the problem, a situation analysis, specification of target audiences (publics), messages to be communicated, and specific program elements to be used, a timetable and budget, discussion of how the program will be evaluated.
      3.   Execution of the campaign means deciding how the message should be communicated to the public(s) of interest. For example, news conferences, sponsorship of charity events, or creating attention-getting promotions.
         Press Release--Information distributed to the media by an organization about its activities, intended to appear as publicity. Common types include: timely topics, research stories, and consumer information.

III. SALES PROMOTIONS--A program designed to build interest in or encourage purchase of a product during a specified time period. Sale promotions focus on more short-term objectives.
  A. Trade Promotions
     1. Discounts and Deals--A manufacturer can reduce a channel partner's costs through sales promotions that give a discount on its own products.
        Merchandise Allowance--Reimburses the retailer for in-store support of the product.
        Case Allowance--A discount to the retailer or wholesaler based on the volume of product ordered.
     2. Industry Boosting and Boasting
        Trade Shows--Events at which many companies set up elaborate exhibits to show their products, give away samples, distribute product literature, and troll for new business contacts.
        Promotional Products--Free products (i.e., coffee mugs, key chains, etc.) that are used to build awareness for the sponsor.
        Incentive Programs--Designed to motivate a firm's own sales force.
        Push Money--A bonus paid by a manufacturer to a salesperson for selling its product.
  B. Consumer Promotions
     1. Price-Based Consumer Promotions--Coupons, price deals, refunds, and rebates.
        Rebates--Sales promotions that allow the customer to recover part of the product's cost from the manufacturer.
        Special Packs--A separate product given away along with another product.
     2. Attention-Getting Consumer Promotions--Stimulate interest in and publicity for a company's products.
        Contests and Sweepstakes--A contest is a test of skill and a sweepstakes is based on chance.
        Premiums--An item included without charge when a consumer buys a product.
        Sampling--Distributing trial-size versions of a product for free to encourage people to try it.
        Point-of-Purchase (POP) Promotion--The use of signs or displays to influence purchases at the store level.
        Cross-Promotion--Two or more products or services combine forces to create interest using a single promotional tool.

IV. PERSONAL SELLING--The part of the promotion mix that involves direct contact between a company representative and a customer.
  A.   The Role of Personal Selling
        Telemarketing--The use of the telephone to sell directly to consumers and business customers.
        Order Taker--A salesperson whose primary function is to facilitate transactions that are initiated by the customer.
        Technical Specialist--Sales support personnel with a high level of technical expertise who assists in product demonstrations.
        Missionary Salesperson--A salesperson who promotes the firm and tries to stimulate demand for a product but does not actually complete a sale.
        Order Getter--A salesperson who works creatively to develop relationships with customers or to generate new sales.
  B.   Approaches to Personal Selling--The evolution from a transactional, hard-sell marketing approach to a relationship approach.
        1.   Transactional Marketing: Putting on the Hard Sell
              Transactional Selling--A form of personal selling that focuses on making an immediate sale with little or not attempt to develop a relationship with the customer.
        2.   Relationship Selling: Countering the Tarnished Image
              Relationship Selling--A form of personal selling in which the salesperson seeks to develop a mutually satisfying relationship with the consumer so as to work together to satisfy each other's needs.
  C.   The Role of Personal Selling in the Promotion Mix--The salesperson's job can be made easier with support from publicity and advertising.
  D.   The Selling Process--The series of activities necessary to bring about a transaction.
        Creative Selling Process--The process of seeking out customers, analyzing needs, determining how product attributes might provide benefits for the customer, and then communicating that information.
        1.   Prospect Customers
              Prospecting--A part of the selling process that includes identifying and developing a list of potential or prospective customers.
        2.   Qualify Prospects--A part of the selling process that determines how likely prospects are to become customers.
        3.   Do a Preapproach--A part of the selling process that includes developing information about prospective customers and planning the sales

interview.

4. Make the Approach--The first step of the actual sales presentation in which the salesperson tries to learn more about the customer's needs, create a good impression, and build rapport.

5. Make the Sales Presentation--The part of the selling process in which the salesperson seeks to persuasively communicate the product's features and the benefits it will provide after the sale.

6. Overcome Customer Objections--Reasons why the prospect is unwilling to commit to a purchase, and the salesperson is prepared to overcome objections by providing additional information or persuasive arguments.

7. Close the Sale--The stage of the selling process in which the salesperson actually asks the customer to buy the product.

8. Follow-up After the Sale--Sales activities that provide important services to the customers.

E. Sales Management--The process of planning, implementing, and controlling the personal selling function of an organization.

1. Setting Sales Force Objectives--What the sales force is expected to accomplish and when.

2. Creating a Sales Force Strategy--How the firm will structure, determine the size, and compensate its sales force.
Sales Territory--A set of customers often defined by geographic boundaries, for whom a particular salesperson is responsible.

3. Recruiting, Training, and Rewarding Salespeople
Recruiting--Attracting and hiring the right set of people to do the job is a top priority for sales managers.
Sales Training--Allows salespeople to learn about the organization and its products and to develop selling skills.
Rewarding Salespeople--Common payment systems used to motivate salespeople include: a straight commission plan, a commission-with-draw plan, and a quota-bonus plan.

CHAPTER 18
ANSWERS

KEY TERMS

1. Sales promotions
2. Merchandize allowance

MULTIPLE CHOICE

1. d
2. a

3. Qualify prospects	3. b
4. Premiums	4. d
5. Point-of-purchase (POP)	5. b
6. Coupons	6. c
7. Order getter	7. a
8. Price deal	8. c
9. Rebate	9. b
10. Telemarketing	10. d
11. Trade promotion objectives	11. a
12. Order taker	12. d
13. Public relations	13. c
14. Publicity	14. a
15. Press release	15. b

CHAPTER IN REVIEW - WRITING TO LEARN

1. Sales promotions assist marketing efforts by creating short-run changes in product sales, by cementing relationships with retailers and wholesalers, and by encouraging high levels of store traffic. Sales promotions also have some less attractive characteristics: they dilute brand equity, they teach consumers always to look for special offers, their effect is only temporary, and they often reach only current users.

2. Sales promotions aimed at industry members and retailers are called trade promotions. Sometimes trade promotions mean manufacturers work to help make retailers more successful by providing local advertising support, conducting sales training or giving the retailer a price allowance. Trade promotions aimed at salesforces and members of industries include trade shows where manufacturers can showcase their products for many buyers from around the country, specialty advertising, and incentive programs such as sales contests.

3. A public relations campaign begins with examining the current attitudes of various publics, determining the issues of interest, and then planning what action to take. A PR campaign may include sponsorship of an event, cause-related marketing activities, and/or developing print or video news releases about timely topics. As with other promotion tools, careful implementation and evaluation are important also.

A CASE ANALYSIS EXERCISE

1. BMW has opened its first full manufacturing facility in the United States.

2.   Bunny Richardson is coordinator for media relations at BMW Manufacturing Corporation.

3.   The BMW Manufacturing Corporation builds the Z3 and M roadsters as well as the Z3 and M coupes for 100 markets throughout the world.

4.   Bunny Richardson began her journalism career in 1973 as a reporter for newspapers in South Carolina and worked as assistant city editor, city editor, and assistant managing editor.

5.   Bunny Richardson joined the BMW manufacturing Corporation as coordinator for community relations in January 1995.